HELPING KIDS

NOT JUST SURVIVE,

AFTER TRAUMA

ALISON NEIHARDT, LPC

Helping Kids to Thrive, Not Just Survive, After Trauma

By Alison Neihardt, LPC

Mission Point Press
2554 Chandler Road
Traverse City, Michigan 49696
Tel.: 231-421-9513
www.MissionPointPress.com

Printed in the United States of America.

Cover and book design by Sarah Meiers

ISBN: 978-1-954786-72-1
Library of Congress Control Number: 2022900979

ALISON NEIHARDT, LPC

MISSION POINT PRESS

Table of Contents

My Mission

Helping kids is my calling, not just the name of my business. I love children. I always have. I began babysitting at the age of twelve and have worked with children ever since. I love helping children and their families. This is my life work. I have worked as a teacher, children's ministry director, missionary, Sunday school teacher, vacation Bible school director, and now counselor.

I see hurting and struggling children and I just want to reach out and help. It could be a problem they are having at home, someone may be hurting them, or they are having a hard time in school. I just want to help them make it better.

Every week in Sunday school class, I do a check-in with my kiddos. This allows them time to tell me what is going on in their lives. They know I will listen to them. They also know that I am interested in them. Even after many years of teaching Sunday school, I still have kids who come to me when they are having a problem or to just get a hug.

I often get asked if I have children. No, I do not, but the kids who come through my door, whether in my office or my Sunday school classroom, are "my" kids. I do my best to look after them. That saying, "It takes a village," is so very true. My church parents know if there is something serious going on with their kids and I find out about it, I will most definitely let them know.

Why am I telling all of this? First, it is what is on my heart, and second, I take the scripture of Jesus letting the little children come to Him very seriously. We need to be like Jesus and let the children come to us. We need to be approachable. Kids need to know they can come to us when they need help. They need to know they have grown-up friends who love them and care about them.

As adults, we need to invest in the lives of children on a daily basis, whether as a parent, grandparent, aunt, uncle, or friend. Kids need to know they matter. We want children to be successful adults, so we adults need to help them.

Some kids go through so much, and they have a hard time trusting adults around them. We need to be an adult they can trust. We may be the only one. It is possible to overcome the hurt, pain, and trauma that happens to kids, with the right people there helping. It needs to be our mission to invest in children in a positive way to help them become successful adults.

CHAPTER

1

THE TRAUMA OF TRAUMA

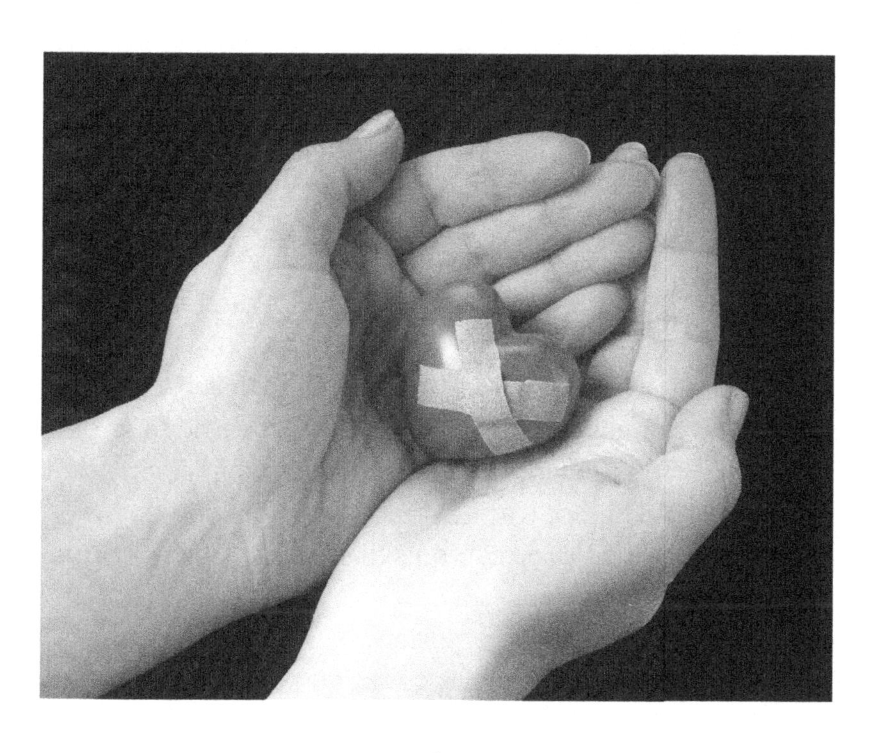

What Is Trauma?

The word trauma sometimes gets overused. We need to think of what trauma really is. It can mean so many different things to different people. For some people, trauma refers to a major physical injury. To others, trauma is emotional or mental, such as death or abuse.

Physical trauma or injury is something that is easy to see. You can tell someone has a broken bone or a large cut. The injury can be mended and healed. An emotional or mental trauma is harder to see.

Mental trauma is something that leaves scars on the inside. They come out as anger, depression, anxiety, or behavior issues. It is a trauma that can take years to even become aware of, let alone treated.

Just like a physical injury can leave scars, so can a mental injury. The scars are just as real. They leave permanent reminders of what happened. Trauma does not just heal itself. If we try to just let it heal or ignore it, the trauma never really goes away. It most likely will not heal correctly.

Trauma can cause heartache and pain no one sees from the outside. It is so painful to even talk about; most of the time, people just bury how they feel and keep secrets for years.

The problem with this is that it does come back. Many childhood traumas are much easier to work through as children, rather than trying to work through them as an adult. By the time a child of trauma reaches adulthood, they most likely have learned poor coping skills and have poor boundaries with others.

Many people who have experienced trauma are just trying to survive. They are trying to cover up pain and hurt. They are so busy trying to survive they are not living. They are not enjoying life.

Part of dealing with trauma is that it changes life forever. Life gets totally dumped upside down. Then one is left trying to figure out how to put the pieces back together. This is true at any age.

When kids go through trauma, they are more likely to thrive and move beyond if they have at least one stable adult who is willing to step in to help and guide them.

No matter what kind of trauma you have gone through, physical or emotional, you need time to heal. After you break a bone, you wear a cast and sometimes use crutches. This gives that bone extra support to help it heal.

When going through an emotional trauma, people need extra support too, sometimes for many years. They have pain that cannot be seen easily. They try to hide it. They only share with a select few the pain they truly have. If they share with you, take it as a compliment and respect them for it. They are reaching out for help not only to survive, but to thrive.

Little People and Scary Stuff

You are a little kid and your parents are fighting and yelling and maybe even hurting each other. You are alone because the person who is supposed to take care of you is too busy drinking or getting high. Your basic needs are not being met. If you cry, you will get hurt or screamed at. You are left to fend for yourself.

Unfortunately, these scenarios happen all too often. Some little kids are exposed at a very young age to traumatic things. They are hurt and scared. There is not an adult there to care for them. They go without food or clothes or other basic needs.

These little ones are always on edge because they have learned to be in order to survive. If they cry, they get hurt. Even though they can speak, they do not, because they are afraid to. They may be malnourished or neglected in other ways as well.

When trauma happens at an early age, it affects these little ones for the rest of their lives. They may have attachment issues, meaning they are afraid to be around anyone because their first caregivers hurt them. They are scared to bond with anyone. They most likely have developmental delays because they do not have anyone who taught them or cared for them like they should have had.

Most of the time the only way to get the trauma to end is for a child protective services agency to get involved. The children are usually removed and placed in foster care. This in itself is traumatic, because their caregiver is taken from them. Eventually, they are able to recover and catch up from their delays. They will hopefully be adopted by someone who can actually care for them.

Even if this all happens, these little ones will have issues for a long time. They will be afraid of things, people, and surroundings for a while. They are scared they will be hurt again.

Being a caregiver for these little ones who have experienced trauma is not easy. It will take time, a lot of patience, understanding, and above all, love. Let them be little. Let them cry, let them play, play with them, and teach them. Show them what a loving parent should be. They deserve it and need it!

Helping these little ones to thrive takes a special person who can be their advocate. They need someone who will step in and protect them from further harm. They need someone who will fight for them. They need someone who can love them.

They have seen a lot of scary stuff in their short lives. They need to be with someone who is safe and not scary. They need someone who will help them be little kids and take proper care of them. This will help them to not only survive, but thrive.

I Do Not Understand

I do not understand. I do not get it. Why would someone want to hurt another person, especially a child? Children are innocent. Why would someone hurt a child? I hear these things being said all the time. I often ask these things in my own mind. I see children who are hurting in my office every day.

We hear horror stories on the news about children being abused. We get angry or feel sad. We want answers. We read or hear that when someone grows up being abused, they often become abusers themselves. Or someone may have an anger problem they cannot control so they take it out on others.

There are so many factors involved in the "why" of abuse. What we need to figure out are ways to not only help the abused child, but also the person who is the abuser. There may be issues in their lives that contributed to them being an abuser. Maybe they were abused. Of course, the person who is the abuser needs to want the help. If they do not want help, then we need to find ways of keeping their victims away from them.

Somehow, the cycle needs to be broken. Helping the victims heal so they learn how to be better people is a good way to start. Then we must help them understand the right way to handle their emotions and understand that hurting another person is not the answer.

We need to teach the victims to not be victims anymore. We need to help them understand what healthy relationships look like. They need to also know what a parent does to properly discipline and interact with their children. They need to know what love and care look like not only for themselves, but also for others around them.

Children need to learn how to properly handle their emotions. They need to learn to trust adults again. This can be a long process. Children who have been abused do not easily trust.

Part of helping childhood victims of abuse is helping them learn from their past and being able to heal. This will help them move on in life and be better people no matter their age.

Childhood trauma affects people well into their adulthood and, for many, a lifetime. It is a matter of being able to heal from it and treat the next generation better than the way they were treated. It takes a lot of work and patience, but in the end, it is so worth the journey to help kids learn to thrive and not just survive trauma.

The Heart of Trauma

The heart, or bottom line, of trauma is that someone has been hurt in some way or another. They have experienced something life changing—whether someone actually hurt them physically, mentally, emotionally, or sexually, or they have been a witness to something. Then there is trauma that just happens, like someone close to them, perhaps a parent, dying.

People who have been through trauma do not need to compare who has had the worst trauma. It is not a competition. It is life. If someone has gone through trauma, even a similar trauma to what you have gone through, be there for them as a support, not a source of competition. Trauma is not a race.

Try to have empathy and understanding for those who have gone through something traumatic—be understanding, be supportive, and offer a listening ear and a shoulder to lean on.

Helping anyone thrive through trauma means being a support, not a hindrance. In a world where hurt and pain are everywhere, be a source of comfort. Childhood victims of abuse, whether they are still children or now grown adults, still carry parts of their trauma with them, some more than others, but it is still there.

Telling someone who has been through trauma to "get over it" does not work. If anything, you are pushing them away. Telling someone to just "get over it" is like telling someone with diabetes to "get over it."

There are things people who have gone through trauma will carry with them forever. It is a matter of learning how to get past it, not "over it." Having patience and understanding is part of helping kids to thrive, not just survive, after trauma. Kids who have gone through trauma behave the way they do because that is how they have functioned day to day.

We as helpers need to understand this and be able to step in and help when someone is struggling. You may not even understand why they are struggling; you can just see it on their face. Do not be afraid to ask questions to help better understand their situation. Be a listening ear to their hurt and pain. Help them so they can see life in a better light.

Even adults who have gone through trauma do revert from time to time, or all the time, to when they were children. They do not trust, they trust the wrong people, and they are taken advantage of. They mess up. Be there as a support to help them pick themselves back up, refocus, and move on.

CHAPTER

2

THE TRAUMAS OF CHILDHOOD

Sticks and Stones

"Sticks and stones may break my bones, but words will never hurt me." How truly wrong is this statement. Kids are dying because they are being bullied so badly. They are being called horrible names. They are being told to just go and die. They are being told they are worthless and should just go kill themselves.

This has to stop. Adults need to be aware of what is happening and put a stop to it. The scars of being bullied last a lifetime. A bully takes down self-esteem. They take away self-respect and self-worth, all with their words. We give bullies too much power.

It gets to the point that kids are afraid to go to school because of these bullies. Kids who are being bullied want to get back at their bullies. So, what do they do? They may punch them or get into some other physical fight. Then the person being bullied gets into trouble because they fought back, and the bully gets away.

How is this fair? The hurt and pain of being bullied is something that carries on into adulthood. If those who were bullied do not learn to stand up for themselves, then the adult bullies will just continue their mistreatment.

When a child is being bullied, they are told to go tell an adult. What if the adult does not do anything? Then the bully thinks they can get away with it. Adults need to step in and deal with the bullies and make it clear that bullying behavior will not be tolerated.

Kids are even being bullied online. They cannot get away. They get messages on social media. They are being talked about by others online. As adults, we need to be aware of what is happening—check your child's social media pages and read their text messages.

If your child is the bully, do not make excuses for them. Do not let them get away with their behavior. If your child is the one being bullied, listen to them. Help them learn to stand up for themselves. Help them when they have tried all they can to get things to stop.

Being bullied is traumatic. It is hard to deal with. It makes school not enjoyable. It affects self-esteem, confidence, and self-worth. We as adults, no matter your role with children, need to step in and help end this epidemic. Kids are dying because of bullying.

Dying Young

Death at any point in life is sad. Death of anyone we love is sad. The death of a parent, however, is one of the scariest things that can happen to a child. When a parent dies, a child has not only lost a parent, they have lost one of their main caregivers and someone who provided for them.

Yes, death is part of life, but to lose a parent at a young age is one of the most painful traumas that could happen to a child. This event affects the rest of their life. This is especially true if the child was being raised by a single parent.

Kids ask questions such as, "Who will care for me?" and "Will my other parent die too?" They feel alone. They hurt. It is so painful they cannot even talk about it and to even think about it brings them to tears and sadness. It seems so unfair. It is something that no one can really understand. Again, they question, "Why did they die?" and "Why did they leave me?"

All kinds of things go through the minds of these children. They blame themselves. They blame the other parent. They blame God. While these are normal parts of the grief process, it just seems worse because it is a child who is grieving.

Helping children through grief is not easy. Life will never be normal again. Establishing a new "normal" is the hard part. Keeping routine is key. Things like bedtime, going to school, and seeing friends and family is all helpful. It not only helps as a routine, but also as a distraction.

Retaining other key supports is also helpful. These people could be family, friends, church family, teachers, and other professionals. Seeking other helpers is also useful. Finding a good therapist or grief group is important. This allows children to grieve with someone who is not going to sit and cry with them.

Many kids do not cry or show sadness because they know the other adults around them are sad so they think they need to "be strong" for them. This is so far from the truth. They need to be able to talk and grieve just like the adults. They need to see it is okay to grieve and be sad.

It is also helpful to provide some distraction. When things settle down, finding things to do as a family to bond and heal is helpful. This could be something like having family nights or having other family activities planned. Take a vacation, go camping, or do something new as a family. Creating new memories will help the healing process.

Do not ever rush anyone's grief—everyone handles grief differently. Do not tell a child or anyone who is grieving to "just get over it." This just creates more problems. It puts a time limit on grieving. Usually the first year after a death is the hardest. It is facing all the firsts of a new normal.

Grief is a curious thing. It creeps in when you least expect it. A girl may wonder who will give her away at her wedding or take her to the daddy-daughter dance. A boy may wish his dad was there to teach him how to fix things.

The pain of a parent dying will never completely go away. Children who have lost a parent need extra love, support, and grace. Try to put yourself in their shoes. Try to understand their feelings and offer comfort and love. Be a listening ear. These children need someone who will hear them.

Keep Your Hands to Yourself

Those of us who work with kids say this pretty much on a daily basis. We tell them it is not nice to hit others. It is not okay to throw things. Then kids look around at adults and try to figure out why adults do the things they as children are told not to.

Trying to explain why daddy hurts mommy is something even harder for a child to understand. I talk to kids all the time who have parents who hurt each other. The children feel scared. They think their parent is mean. They are mad. They try to step in and protect their parent from getting hurt.

No child should witness violence between their parents. This is a trauma that carries on in life well into adulthood. Kids who grow up witnessing this believe this is normal behavior. They think it is okay to hit their spouse and it is okay to be hit; they get involved in a relationship where the cycle just continues.

How sad is it for kids to think that violence is part of a "normal" relationship? Then kids try to understand why the parent who is being mistreated stays. "Why would my mom stay with a man who hurts her? It just does not make sense." They are right—it does not.

They are wise beyond their years. It does not make sense that adults would be so angry with each other that they would hit each other. Kids grow up in these environments and are confused, hurt, and scared.

I hear kids tell me things that happen in their homes that are just so scary for a child to listen to and be a part of. How traumatic it would be to have the police called to your house because mom and dad are fighting and hurting each other.

Even scarier yet is if the child is taken away from their parents because of the fighting and physical harm. The child is placed in foster care or with another family member because they witnessed their parents hurt each other.

Domestic violence happens at every economic and educational level, in all walks of life. We need to be more aware of it and help the victims get the help they need to get away. This includes the young victims. I know of children who have tried to get in the middle of their parents' fighting and gotten hurt too.

Kids need to feel safe in their homes. They need to feel safe from hurt and violence. It is the job of the parents and adults in their lives to make sure this is the case. Kids go through enough in their young lives; they do not need to watch or be part of their parents fighting with each other.

We adults need to take our own instruction and advice. Keep your hands to yourselves. Our hands can be used for so many other things besides hurting others. Let's use them to help, not hurt.

Don't Mess with My Mama!

Many children who grow up with a single mom feel this way. They go to great lengths to "protect" their moms. This is especially true for boys. If or when mom dates, even if the boy is young, they feel the need to protect their mother from getting hurt.

They may even try to cause problems so mom does not

date. If your child says they do not like someone you are dating, listen to them. Listen to their reasons. Kids are pretty good at reading people.

In cases of domestic violence, boys are more likely to try to stop the fight or step in between their mom and the person trying to hurt her. While this is a protective and noble gesture, it is one that could end very badly for all involved.

The child could also get hurt, or the fight could escalate into something way worse. The best thing children can do when their mom is being hurt is to call for help—lock themselves in a closet with a phone and dial 911 or go to a neighbor and call for help.

Children need to know their parent is safe. They feel, because there is not another protector in the house, it is their job to protect. This is all well and good but could cause some serious issues really quickly in a case of domestic violence.

If a child has been involved in a domestic violence case, they are less likely to be as trusting of the next man who comes into their mother's life. Or they just figure it is normal for this to happen. Either way it is not good.

The best course of action, as hard as it may be, is for the mother to get out of the abusive relationship. She and her children need to be safe. Children need to feel safe in their own home. They also need to know the ones they love and care for the most are safe.

This is helping kids to thrive, not just survive, after trauma. Kids who have experienced abusive relationships, whether as a witness or being abused themselves, have scars and pain that can last well into adulthood.

If you are in a relationship that has been abusive, you need to get out and get help and so do your children. Even if it is "just" emotional or verbal abuse, abuse is abuse. You and your children deserve better in this life.

If you know someone who is in an abusive situation, offer to help. Leaving that kind of relationship is difficult and the person will need a lot of support and grace while they are leaving and trying to put their lives back together. Do not get frustrated if they talk about going back or actually go back to the abuser. This is pretty normal behavior.

Also, keep in mind their past. The person you are trying to help may have been or most likely was abused some other time in their lives. There are many pieces to helping someone who has been abused. It takes a long time to put things right again. Do not give up on them.

Helping kids to understand domestic violence and work through what has happened to them and their parent is helping them thrive, not just survive.

Please Stop Yelling

We have all been there. We have lost it and yelled, often at a loved one. Sometimes, people go to the extent of using threatening words or gestures. People use inappropriate words and say hurtful things in the middle of being angry.

The problem comes when this becomes a pattern—yelling over little things, yelling at someone we love over things that seem so little on a daily basis, threatening to leave them, break their things, or hurt them physically. This behavior crosses a line ... a big line.

This is not how we should be treating others or allow someone to treat us. Yelling all the time does not solve the problem. It just creates another one. It creates fear. It also creates a living environment that is not healthy. People walk around on eggshells, worried they will set off the person who yells.

Usually, if someone does this much yelling, they have other

issues with anger. They explode at almost anything they don't like. They go from zero to sixty in their anger for no reason.

Even when adults yell, thinking there are no kids around, kids still hear it. They hear what is being said. They are scared. They hide. They cry. They are scared of the person who yells.

When someone uses yelling as a tactic for gaining control over someone else, this is verbal and emotional abuse. This is harder to prove or see because the marks are not visible. However, verbal and emotional abuse can and most of the time does lead to some kind of physical abuse.

Kids who experience this grow up thinking this behavior is okay. They do not realize this is not normal behavior. They grow up being scared. When they become adults, they yell to get what they want too. The cycle continues.

If someone has this much anger and yells all the time, they need help. Some, however, do not see they have an issue. They think the victim is being disrespectful or overexaggerating.

Being in a relationship like this is toxic. It is toxic for the adult and the children involved. If you are in this situation, I encourage you to get out and stay out. You and your children deserve better.

Growing up in an emotionally and verbally abusive home causes scars that last a lifetime. They are just harder to see because they are not physical. You and your children are being hurt by staying in an emotionally and verbally abusive relationship.

Help kids thrive, not just survive. Get out of an abusive relationship. Reach out for help. Cut ties with the abuser as much as you can. This is not what God has intended for you or your children.

Parenting from Jail

Everyone makes mistakes, even parents. For some parents, it is a short-term incident of sitting in jail for a few days. Some parents end up in prison for the rest of their lives. Whatever the case, a parent going to jail for committing a crime is a scary thing.

Kids do not understand how their parent could make such a big mistake or hurt someone and do something to break the law. I try to explain it to my client kiddos in this way. We talk about the fact mom or dad made a mistake. They made a bad choice. This choice means they have to go to jail. Jail is like time-out for adults.

When a parent goes to jail, it is a traumatic event, no matter the reason. The children are separated from their parent. They worry about their parent being gone. They worry something might happen to their parent while they are in jail. Kids are angry because their parent did something so wrong to put them in jail.

Some kids are relieved their parent is in jail because their parent hurt them or someone close to them. They are afraid of their parent and know jail is a place that keeps them safe from their parent. They still love and miss their parent, but they are angry.

The trauma of trying to understand why their parent would hurt someone and do harmful things is something no kid should ever have to come to terms with. "Why would my parents do something so stupid like sell drugs and end up in jail?" "Why would my parent hurt someone?" "Why would my parent hurt me?"

A parent in jail also means life changes drastically for the children involved. The children end up living with other family members or end up in foster care. Their whole life gets turned upside down. They may be separated from siblings. They may end up living with people they do not know. All of these things are scary and traumatic to say the least.

Some cases are in the media, so trying to keep kids from seeing what happened is harder yet. Then others talk about the situation and your child overhears it. Not good ... more trauma that just keeps going.

Helping these children who have a parent in jail is not easy. Helping them understand the best they can and at their level is not an easy thing to do. Helping children adjust to having their parent in jail for so long that they may not see them again until they are grown is difficult for children to understand.

Kids feel abandoned by their parent. They are ashamed because their parent is in jail. They feel angry and afraid. Kids need to feel reassured they did not do anything wrong. They need to understand that their parent will be okay. Their parent is getting help while they are in jail.

If the parent can get mail, encourage your child to write to their parent. Encourage them to say how they feel. Reach out and get professional supports in place to help your child during this time in their lives. Kids can go beyond the issues related to a parent in jail with the proper supports. Help these children thrive.

Can't You Just Kiss and Make Up?

Kids ask this or similar questions when they first find out their parents are getting a divorce. Some kids are relieved to a point when they find out their parents are getting a divorce, but divorce is hard on everyone involved.

Kids do not feel like they have control over what is

happening. They are right—they do not. They hear fighting all the time. Kids tell me a major frustration is when their parents fight over them. They feel like they are in the middle and do not like being fought over.

During a divorce, parents can use the kids as messengers to tell the other parent information. Some parents also use the kids as a way to get back at the other parent or as a pawn in the divorce.

All of these things cause major stress on kids. Please, for the love of God, stop. Do not do this to your kids. These are the things that cause trauma and anxiety. Let your kids love both parents. Do not put them in the middle. Do not make them choose sides.

Your kids are having a hard-enough time with what is happening and do not need more stress and drama added to the mess. Divorces are messy enough without adding more to it. Kids just want their parents to get along and love each other again.

Divorce is a traumatic enough problem. Yes, divorce seems more and more common, but it does not make it any less traumatic. A child's world is being dumped upside down. Their life and everything they know is changing.

What kids need during this time is support. They need adults, family, and friends to support them. To help them. To show and tell them they are still loved. Kids need reassurance that everything will be okay. They need to know it is not their fault.

Divorce has long-term, life-altering effects on children. It does not matter how old they are—it still affects them. They grow up going between homes. They have to share holidays with their parents. They worry a lot. They worry if their parents will fight. They worry if their parents will show up to events. They worry about the transition between homes. They worry all the time.

Helping kids of a divorce is no easy task. Divorce is messy ... sometimes really messy. Sometimes parents just plain disappear. They leave with no reason. Kids are left feeling abandoned.

Divorce creates a life that becomes unstable. There is a lot of change. The parent that stayed at home now goes back to work. There most likely will be moving to a new home at least once.

During this time of instability, kids need as much structure and routine as possible. They need to still have rules and schedules. This helps life be more normal. Hopefully the divorce situation stabilizes and the kids adjust to a new normal. Life gets into a routine. Things settle down and they get used to life in a different way.

During this time, kids can regress developmentally. They can become extra emotional. Their feelings go all over the place. Just be patient and listen. Be there to support them and love them through their pain.

Divorce is messy. It is big. It is scary. Helping kids through a divorce is no easy task. It takes help. It takes support. It takes a listening ear and an open mind. Try to be these things to kids going through a divorce. Help them come through the other side and thrive.

Money Well Spent

Children and money always seem to go hand and hand. Children have needs—food, clothes, a place to live, schooling, and the list goes on forever. It is never-ending. One of the major parts of being a responsible parent is providing physically for your child.

Some parents, however, seem to be missing this part of

being a parent. They see paying child support as something that is not needed or necessary. They just see it as another bill they need to avoid. They use not paying child support as a way of getting back at the other parent. That is not the case, or at least, it should not be. Child support is helping to pay for the things your child needs to live.

By paying child support, you are helping to care for the day-to-day needs of your child—the child you helped to create. Look at it as an investment in the future—your child's future.

It is not someone else's job to care for your child and their needs. Paying child support is a necessity. There are so many children living below the poverty level because their parent refuses to pay child support.

Children know if their parent is paying child support. They figure it out. They know things cost money. They know that if their parent is not paying child support, this affects them directly. For instance, they can get a new pair of shoes or not, or they can get new clothes or not. These are things that children should not even know about, let alone worry about. But they do.

Please step up and take responsibility for your child. Be present. Be active. Provide for their needs. They should not have to worry how they are going to get the things they need. They should not have to worry about if they have a place to live or not. These are worries for adults, not children.

Take your child to get the things they need. Child support only goes so far. If they need shoes, go buy them shoes. If they need clothes, buy them clothes. Children are depending on their parents to provide for them.

Children see not paying child support as their parent not loving them. There is no other way to explain it. They do not understand why their parent cannot provide for their needs.

It turns into a trust issue. Do not make promises to do

things or get them things and not keep the promise. Children trust their parent more than any other person in their lives. Do not break their trust by not providing for them.

When children go without the things they need, this affects them both in the short term and the long term. Help your child to thrive, not just survive.

I'm Hungry

"Mom, I'm hungry," is a statement every mother hears many times a day. Kids are always hungry. They are growing children. Now imagine your child telling you they are hungry and you do not have anything in your cupboard to feed them. You work all the time and still cannot make ends meet.

You do not have enough food to feed your family and struggle to meet their basic needs. Maybe you are or have even been homeless. For many families, wondering where their next meal is coming from is a daily struggle.

Poverty is something that is very hard to overcome. It is hard to break the cycle of being poor and growing up poor. This is a form of trauma. Basic needs are not met and worries abound about how they will be met. For many kids, this is all too real of a situation.

There could be several reasons for the poverty. The child may be growing up in a single-parent home and the parent works all the time and still cannot seem to make ends meet. The parent may be neglecting the child for their own problems, ranging from substance use to gambling to mental illness.

In order to survive, the child may steal food from other kids at school or go to a friend's house every night for dinner. If the child is old enough, they might get a job so they can buy their own food.

There are many programs in place to help families in these situations. They give out food, clothes, and help with other basic needs. While the programs help to fill in the gap, what is especially needed is someone to help them, one-on-one, break the cycle of poverty. There are many factors that play into this cycle.

For many families, it is generational. It has gone on for years and they just feel stuck. They want to get out, but they just do not know how. They need someone who can help them learn to do things to break this cycle, such as:

- Teach better money management strategies
- Help the next generation fill out applications for college
- Help the adults develop a new skill set to get another job that pays better
- Help adults fill out job applications and practice job interview skills

These things take time. It takes someone who has patience and understanding to help these families. Sometimes it is just a matter of the children needing to be removed because of the neglect.

Living at the poverty level is a hard way to grow up. It can be very traumatic—losing a home not just once, but many times; not having basic needs met which makes it difficult to learn in school and not worry about other things like food and clothes; or having adults at home who value education and can help with schoolwork.

To help break this cycle, are you willing to step in and help? Can you offer your professional services for free, in order to help families be able to move out of poverty into a life where they feel safe and stable? Imagine if we all did this? How great things would be in our communities.

Growing Up Addicted

Kids are told all the time that drugs and alcohol are not good for them. Drugs make them do things that could harm them or someone else. What happens if a child is the one who gets harmed by their parent who uses drugs or alcohol? The parent can get mean or abusive or spend all their money on drugs or alcohol instead of food. The parent may even go as far as selling the child's gifts to get money to support their addiction. How heartbreaking, right?

Children of an addict learn, at a young age, that they not only have to take care of themselves but others in the house too. This includes their addict parent. Children are going without basic necessities such as food, shelter, clothes, and education because of a parent's addiction.

Then there is the situation where kids are being mistreated, abused, or neglected because of their parent's addiction. Kids walk on eggshells so they do not upset their parent for fear of getting in trouble or getting hurt.

Kids are not allowed to be kids. They are too worried about taking care of others around them. They do not invite friends over because they are afraid and embarrassed to do so. Kids struggle in school because there is not help at home or they are too busy caring for others to do schoolwork.

All of this leads to issues not only in childhood but also into adulthood. Children who grow up in this environment think this is normal. As an adult, they could even marry an addict or become an addict themselves.

These things are traumatic on so many levels for children, causing so many fears and anxieties. Children do not understand why their parent picks drugs or alcohol over them. They do not understand why their parent does not want them or cannot take care of them.

Many of these children end up in the foster care system or living with other family members because their parent cannot take care of them. This is so hard on these children. They feel like they are not wanted or important.

Helping children of addicts to thrive is to help them see they are important. They can do well despite what their parents have done. They need help to understand it is not their fault that their parent acts the way they do. They need someone who will listen to them and not judge them. They need understanding and reassurance. They need to learn they can thrive, not just survive.

The Broken System

Foster care—the two most feared words by many parents and children. Children in foster care are usually there because of abuse or neglect by a caregiver, usually a parent.

There are never enough foster care parents. There are never enough resources to help these children who have been removed from their families. They were removed from what they knew, but no matter how scary or bad of a situation for that child, it was "normal."

Children who have been removed from their parents and placed in foster care can be placed with several different families. They end up in the court system. They see their parents in a supervised environment for their protection.

All of these things are very traumatic for the children in the foster care system. They need help. They need resources. They need protection. But, above all else, they need love.

Their parents do love them but are so busy dealing with their own issues that they do not know how to show love or care for their child. Their parent has made some very poor choices and their child is paying the consequences.

Not every child stays in foster care. Some get to go back to their parents. This is usually a yearlong process, give or take. Some children are placed back with their parents and then removed again, because the situation reverts to what it was before.

When helping a child who is in the foster care system, keep in mind they may take their time trusting you. They have been hurt. They may not want to talk about what happened to them. They want life to be "normal" again. They want a family—a family who will love them.

They feel broken. They feel abandoned. They are scared. Being removed from their parents is a traumatic event. When a child has been in the system long enough, they begin to not trust the system. They do not trust the courts, social workers, lawyers, and other people involved in the system.

They are tired of telling their "story" so many times to so many people. Every time they have to tell what happened to them, they are reliving the trauma. What they have experienced is enough to make any adult's heart break.

A child in foster care worries about becoming attached to someone because they have had people leave their lives so many times before. They develop attachment issues. As the adult, do not be offended if a child does not become your buddy right away. Let them take their time.

Children in foster care have had to leave a home with only a moment's notice. They have had to place their belongings in garbage bags to leave. Many times, they lose items that are important to them along the way.

Take all of this into consideration when helping a child of foster care. Let them grieve their losses. They have many. Help them understand you are a trusted adult who can help them in their journey.

When helping a child who is phasing out of foster care, help them learn to be an adult. Help them with getting through school and applying for jobs and college. Help them find housing. Be the safe house to come to when they need help. Many children who phase out of foster care become homeless. They have not been taught how to be an adult by anyone.

If you really want to help children of foster care thrive, not just survive, teach them how to be a productive adult. Be their support system. Teach them the things they were never taught growing up, because when they were growing up, they were just trying to survive life.

CHAPTER

3

FEELINGS OF TRAUMA

A Feelings Whirlwind

Feelings and emotions can be very complicated things to understand. Often we have more than one emotion or feeling at the same time. In some cases, our emotions turn into the perfect storm. Our emotions can sometimes really get the better of us. We feel out of control. This is especially true for children.

Children are just learning what their feelings are and what they mean. Then add in trauma on top of that and you have the perfect storm—the perfect storm of emotions. Feelings can be hard to get a grip on, especially for children.

Trauma adds new emotions and levels of hurt. It is so painful to even talk about. But, in the case of trauma and children, the first things that need to be explained are feelings.

Teaching children about their feelings is key, especially for a child who has had trauma. How else are they supposed to communicate how they feel or what they are thinking? When I begin working with a new client kiddo, I begin by teaching them about feelings.

We play feelings games, read feelings books, and look at charts and other visual helps to learn how to identify feelings. Helping kids be able to tell you how they feel is huge. This gives them control.

The next step is to validate how they feel. This helps kids know you are listening and care about their feelings. Their feelings are not wrong. They are their feelings. You may not understand why they feel that way, but they are not wrong in how they feel. God wired all of us, including children, to having feelings. This is what makes us human.

Anyone who has gone through trauma tries to hide their feelings. They have learned to survive day to day by hiding how they truly feel. Kids and people in general with histories of trauma put on a mask to cover how they really feel. The mask is a way to protect them from further harm. It also hides the pain they feel from others.

Kids are sometimes very good at this to a point. Feelings do come out no matter how hard children try to hide them. They come out in anger, during a crying outburst for no apparent reason, or just in general acting-out behavior.

We need to help victims of trauma, both kids and adults, be able to express how they feel. Trauma is something you cannot hide forever. It is like trying to hide a chronic illness. Victims of trauma need a chance to heal from the trauma they have experienced. For many adults, their trauma happened as children.

The best way to help trauma victims is to help them learn their feelings and what they mean. It is also necessary for victims of trauma to be able to express their feelings in a safe, protected environment. Their feelings need to be acknowledged and validated.

All of these things will help calm the storm of feelings they have felt in their lives. The storm of feelings can be a nasty one. God can help with calming this storm in your life. God is the ultimate healer if you let Him. After all, He is the one who created you, feelings and all.

My Kid the Hulk

Does your kid seem to go from zero to sixty in just a few seconds? Do they seem to get angry so fast that you are not even sure where it came from? Do they seem to turn into the Hulk over something so little?

We have all gotten angry at different points in our lives.

We get angry over little things that really do not matter. Kids are no different. They get angry because they feel something is unfair. They get angry because they get their feelings hurt. They get angry because they do not get their way. This anger comes and goes.

Anger becomes a bigger issue when it is constant—when it turns into full-blown meltdowns or when a child cries and screams for no apparent reason. Children can become angry over something little when there are bigger stressors going on—situations they cannot control. These could include a parent leaving, being bullied, divorce, abuse, or fighting at home. All these things cause a lot of stress and trauma in the life of a child.

Many times, children do not know why they are angry or what to do about it. They have meltdowns or outbursts when something is not within their control. When there is trauma going on, there are a lot of things that are not within anyone's control.

Anger is also a sign of anxiety. When we are anxious about something and worry, sometimes that worry turns into fear. Fear turns into anger. When there is something scary going on, kids may have meltdowns because they do not know how to communicate their feelings, or they are afraid to communicate them.

Trying to find out what is causing the anger will help your child. Talk to them. Find out what they are upset about. When kids are upset about something, they may try to change the subject. They may try to be funny or just not talk because it is too painful and upsetting to talk about what is really bothering them.

Most kids have a hard time identifying what is making them angry. They have to think about it. It is really hard for most kids to admit when they are angry with someone they love, like their parent, even if they have very valid reasons for being angry with them.

Children do not want to admit they are angry with a parent because they love their parent so much and they do not want to hurt their parent. Children also do not want to admit they are angry with their parent because they do not want their parent to be angry with them or leave them. This is especially true if there has been some traumatic event that has happened. The child is already upset and worried about their relationship with their parent.

How to help your child through their anger can be tricky. Helping them figure out what is upsetting them is important even if you are the one with whom they are angry. Help them try to resolve the issue as best as possible. It will take a lot of patience, reassurance, and consistency. Sometimes, it may take the help of a professional.

Children will get angry. In most cases, they will just get over it. When they cannot, they may need help to deal with their anger. Kids do not like feeling angry anymore than you as the adult like to see them angry. It is our job to help them not feel like they are going to turn into the Hulk.

My Tummy Hurts

Kids tell mom and dad often that their tummy hurts. Maybe they ate too much junk food. Maybe there is some other medical reason for their stomach pain. When there seems to be no medical reason for their upset stomach, then other reasons need to be explored.

When a child complains of a stomachache or headache and there does not seem to any medical reason behind the pain, it may be time to look at things in your child's life that could be causing stress or anxiety. These things may be small to you or they could be a big traumatic event.

Are there issues at home? Are they having problems at school? Be aware of what is happening in your child's life. Are they complaining of other things? Are they not wanting to go to school? Is there a lot of fighting going on at home? Do they not want to go home? Do they not want to be around a certain person?

After the medical tests are done and no answers are found, talk to your child's doctor about stress and anxiety issues. Talk to your child about what is bothering them. There may be issues of which you are not aware.

What do you do for children who are struggling with anxiety? Help them learn to manage it. Seek out help from a qualified child therapist. They should be able to help your child with their anxiety. Try to get to the bottom of why or what is causing the stress and anxiety.

When I have a client kiddo in my office who has anxiety or a lot of stress, we talk. We talk about what is happening. Many times, the child is not even aware why they are stressed. Sometimes, children put too much pressure on themselves to do well. They think they have to be perfect.

Many times, the reason for the anxiety and stress is a big life stressor, something like a divorce, a death, being bullied, or some other trauma. They worry themselves so much it makes them sick.

How do you help these children? Teach them how to recognize when they are feeling overwhelmed and what to do about it. Talk to them. Help them figure out what relaxes them. Help them figure out who they can go to for help.

Make your child a calming kit. A calming kit is a bin or bag with things in it to help them calm down when they are feeling stressed. Include items like music, coloring, puzzles, play dough, or whatever would help your child relax. Keep it in a place where your child can easily access it, such as by their bed in their room.

Trauma is the biggest cause of anxiety and stress. When life is chaotic or extra stressful, anxiety creeps in. When there is trauma or stress, we do not know which end is up. Life is unpredictable. Life is dumped upside down.

When children are feeling stressed, they have tummy aches and headaches. They may not be sleeping well. They may be having nightmares. They may have meltdowns or outbursts for no apparent reason.

Helping your child get a hold of their anxiety so they can function day to day is key. It is what helps them to not just survive, but thrive.

The Worry Machine

The gears turn. Things spin. They go around and around. Sometimes, these machines never stop. Things just keep going. The same goes with worry. We worry about all kinds of things.

When you were a kid, what did you worry about? Kids now have so many bigger worries. They worry about their parents getting a divorce. They worry someone is going to hurt them or bully them at school. They may even worry whether their basic needs will be met, like food and shelter.

Now add in having a traumatic event like abuse or parents getting a divorce. There are so many stressors that can happen in a child's life that can cause them to worry. Some things just happen that no one has control over, like a death.

Kids worry that when one thing happens, like a death or divorce, other things will happen too. Many times this worry carries over into adulthood. Kids develop issues with anxiety or constant worry.

When kids talk about worry, they may complain of headaches or stomachaches. They may have bad dreams. These are all things to pay attention to. They could be signs of a child having worry or anxiety issues.

Changes in life like a different school or a new baby can also cause worry. Allow your child to express themselves and how they feel. Help them reason out their worries and deal with them, so they do not affect how they function in their day-to-day life. Anxiety can be crippling.

If they are worried about going to school, try to find out why. Is it a teacher or a bully? Help them problem solve in dealing with the situation. Help them feel more organized and able to handle school in a healthy way.

Part of helping a child with worry, no matter how big, is to reassure them and listen. Their worries may not make sense to you, but they do to them. Help them talk and think through it.

Worry goes around and around like a wheel. Sometimes the worry goes really fast and all the time. Sometimes the worry is slow and steady.

God tells us to not worry. He tells us to give Him our worries. Pray with your child when they have a worry, be it about a test or a traumatic event like losing a loved one.

Part of helping a child through worry during a traumatic event is to have as much routine and structure as possible. Sometimes, it is good for kids to go back to school where they do not have to think about the bad stuff that has happened to them.

The worry may not totally go away. As caregivers, we can help a child through their times of worry, stress, and anxiety by listening to them and being there for them. Sometimes a child with worry issues does better by talking to someone not involved in the situation.

Getting proper help for your child who worries is important. When I counsel children, we talk about the worries and I usually ask them if it is a little worry or a big worry. This helps me gauge what they see as a big deal.

This is key to helping your child deal with their anxiety in a healthy way. They need to learn to cope with worries, so they can thrive, not just survive.

Facing Fear with Faith

We are all afraid of something or someone. It may be a fear of spiders, snakes, the dark, or the bogeyman. There is a phobia for everything. Some fears keep us from getting hurt physically. Some fears keep us from living life. We become so afraid that we are scared to live life.

What fears are keeping you from living your life to the fullest? The fear of failing? The fear of getting hurt? The fear of rejection? While these fears are very real, they are also very crippling. We fear because we have been hurt before. How does one get over these fears to move on to living life?

I tell the kids I work with that fear does not come from God. We have to pick ourselves up and move on. Sometimes, that is easier said than done. When we have been hurt deeply, it is hard to trust. It is hard to just "move on" from the pain. We learn from our pain and adjust accordingly.

Kids learn what fear is at an early age. They learn to fear fire because they know they will get hurt. How do we help kids overcome their fears? We help build their confidence. We help build their skills. We help them trust others again.

Some kids have had big hurts in their little lives. They have been hurt, abused, neglected, and mistreated. They think that, for the most part, this is just life and it is normal. But when they are not in that situation, they can see what they thought was normal is really not.

They learn coping skills to deal with avoiding the hurt. They may not get close to another adult again because they do not trust adults. They may not have many friends because they have been bullied.

It is such a sad and lonely way to live life. There are fears we all need to face in life. For some it is a fear of spiders and for others, a fear of rejection. We need to be able to face those fears with faith. Having faith in God to help us face those fears is key. God knows our fears. He tells us to give our fears to Him. He tells us to trust Him. God is our protector. He is our healer.

He helps us face those fears and come out on the other side. Not every adult is going to hurt children. Not every peer is going to bully your child and reject them. Teaching kids how to find safe people—people they can trust—is key. This can be hard when there has been trauma, hurt, and pain.

God calms our fears. He knows who has hurt us and why we might be scared of them. I encourage my client kiddos to talk to God about their fears. We talk about ways to deal with their fears in a healthy way in order to push through them. Pushing through fear is part of life and part of the healing process.

We need to allow God to heal our big hurts. We need to trust Him in the healing process. We need to give God the control to heal our fears in life—little fears and big ones.

You Left Me!

Left behind. Abandoned. Left out. No matter how you put it, being abandoned hurts. There are many times in our lives when we have been left out of some kind of party or activity for any number of reasons. While this is hurtful, it is something most people can push past and move beyond.

Then there are cases where a parent or other significant person has left a child. They have just packed up and moved away, in many cases, for no apparent reason. I have heard many stories of kids whose parents have packed up and left town or the state and left them behind.

The reasons for leaving vary—they leave because of work, they leave because they just want to, or they leave because they have a new significant other in their life. It does not matter the reason. It still hurts. The parents made the choice to leave.

This leaves a very insecure child behind. They are devastated. They are broken because their parent, the one person who should have stayed, did not. Kids become scared and traumatized by this event. They:

- Do not know what to do for themselves
- Do not understand why they were left behind
- Get angry
- Act out
- Become depressed
- Are in so much pain they just close right up
- Do not want to talk about it because of the hurt
- Try different ways of handling the pain—some ways are just not good
- Feel like their parent chose something else over them
- Feel abandoned

- Worry someone else will do the same thing
- Do not get close to anyone else—they are afraid they will be left again and hurt again
- Feel alone
- Push others away to keep themselves safe
- Build walls for protection

This causes issues in other relationships. They have a hard time being close to anyone else. They try to people-please so they will not be left again. They worry they will never see their parent again. They worry about who will take care of them.

Helping kids with this kind of pain takes a lot of love, reassurance, and patience. They have been hurt. Someone close to them left. They do not easily trust adults. It will take time for them to rebuild trust with others around them but trust can be rebuilt eventually.

They may need more one-on-one attention. They may need more help with things. They need a listening ear and a patient heart. Their wound is big. It will not be healed overnight.

Kids also need to understand they do have someone in their lives who will never leave them—God. Their Heavenly Father will never leave them. He will always be with them no matter what happens in life. It also does not matter how much they mess up and the mistakes they make. God loves them unconditionally.

Teaching kids these things help them to not only survive but thrive. They can come through the pain to the other side and be able to go on with life. They can be happy.

More Than Tears

We have all been sad many times in our lives for a variety of reasons. We may be sad when someone dies or when we do not get what we wanted. We may be sad when we get our feelings hurt by someone.

Sadness usually brings a mix of emotions. There are usually tears, anger, frustration, and sometimes just plain depression. We can become depressed for many reasons as well. Depression is a long state of sadness. Nothing feels right. Nothing matters. We do not want to do anything.

Depression usually happens when someone has experienced trauma. There are so many feelings attached to trauma. Emotions come as a big mess. Part of depression is feeling hopeless or even numb.

Kids become depressed just as easily as adults. When a child is depressed, it is hard to know what to do for them or how to help them. Kids tend to act out when they are depressed. They may or may not cry. They may try to cover it up by showing they are happy, when really they are not.

When kids are depressed, they will not want to do things they usually enjoy doing. They may become clingier. They may have problems sleeping. Usually depression and anxiety happen at the same time for kids. They worry about things over which they have no control.

Kids also may become more easily frustrated. They may have more meltdowns. Kids have a hard time recognizing their emotions or why they are upset.

Kids of trauma have had really bad life-altering things happen. Life will never be the same. They are trying to figure out how to function. They are sad because something has happened that is so scary and so difficult.

They have even less control than adults do. Keep this in mind when your kid melts down about something that you see as little and silly—it's not the little thing that upsets them. They are upset about the other stuff they cannot control.

They cannot control going between two homes. They cannot control that someone close to them dies. They cannot control a lot of things in their lives. Try to give them options such as what color shirt to wear or what to have for a snack. These are little things, but your child will, at least hopefully, feel like they have some control.

When kids are depressed, try to help them by reassuring them that things will be okay. Listen to them when they talk even if it is about little stuff. Encourage them to do fun things. Ask them why they feel sad.

Many kids who are depressed need professional help. Find a therapist who works with children, someone who understands childhood depression. Depression is not the same for kids as for adults. There are some things that are similar, but there are also some things that are vastly different.

Helping kids to thrive means helping them with depression—getting them the help they need and teaching them some coping skills to handle the depression they are having. Many times, kids want to talk to someone who is not directly involved in the situation.

Part of healing from trauma is healing from depression and learning how to handle it in the future. This is how to help kids thrive, not just survive.

Safety First

Safety should be the top priority for anyone who works with kids. We take safety precautions every day—we wear seat belts, put our little passengers in car seats, lock the doors, schools screen their employees, and anyone who comes in contact with kids goes through a background check.

All of these things are so important. We need to be aware of who is around our children when they are out of their parents' care. There are some parents who are more aware of these measures than others. Some of these adults are ones who have a child who has experienced trauma.

Their child has already been hurt once or more in their lifetime. So, their parent or guardian is making very sure their child is safe in the care of others. Children who have been through trauma also want to make sure they are safe.

I ask children regularly if they feel safe at home and school. If they tell me no, I ask them why they feel that way. It is usually because something scary has happened to them in those places, or they just do not feel comfortable.

Everyone should feel safe at home. Kids usually have a pretty good sense of who they feel safe with. If they tell you they do not feel safe with someone or they feel uncomfortable, there is usually a reason. Make sure to listen.

If a child does not want to go home, there is usually a reason. It is our job as helpers to find out the reason. Is there fighting going on at home? Is there a problem with someone in the home? Kids will usually feel afraid to tell why. It takes trust for kids to say why they are not feeling safe.

If they are not feeling safe at school it may be for reasons like bullying or a teacher who is giving them a hard time. As a parent or guardian, it is important to find out why. Most kids, at some point, do not want to go to school, just like we adults do not want to go to work on some days. But if it becomes a daily occurrence with a lot of tears and anxiety, then there is a problem that needs to be investigated.

Safety is a major concern for children who have experienced trauma. I regularly reassure my client kiddos and my church kiddos that if they do not feel safe, they need to tell me so I can help them. I also tell them that part of my job is to do my best to help them feel safe. Kids who have experienced trauma need to know they are safe. This usually takes more reassurance and time than for other kids who have not experienced trauma.

How to help a child who has experienced trauma is not easy. We need to show them how we are trying to keep them safe. So, this may literally mean we show them the safety measures we adults take to keep them safe.

I also help families make a safety plan with and for their child. We use things like safe words or phrases. For example, if someone else besides the parent is picking up the child, there is a word or phrase used between adult and child so the child knows it is safe.

Explaining to your child the people who are and aren't allowed to pick them up is also important. If the child has been told someone is not safe to pick them up and that person tries to pick them up, they need to tell an adult immediately. This mainly happens in custody issues.

If the child sees an adult out in public who has been determined as not safe, they need to find an adult immediately. Of course, explaining to your child to never talk to or go with a stranger is also important.

Children of trauma may need this repeated many times. Sometimes they have issues with boundaries due to trauma and need to relearn safe boundaries. Keeping kids safe is the top priority to helping any child of trauma to not just survive, but to thrive.

Feelings Are No Joke

We all enjoy a good joke. It is good to laugh and joke around. Joking has its time and place. However, do not joke about the feelings of someone you care about or who you know is going through a hard time. It comes across as if you do not care about them and what is going on in their lives.

We all have feelings. God created us to have these feelings. From young children to adults, we all have points in our lives that are hard, and our emotions are just a jumbled mess.

This is especially true for a person who has experienced trauma. People, no matter their age or when the trauma happened, have emotions that are hard to deal with and sort out. Their feelings are theirs, no one else's. Validate their feelings. Validate your own feelings. It is okay to have feelings. No one's feelings are wrong, including your own.

God calls us to have compassion for others and walk in their shoes. This is having empathy for someone else. When we make light of or joke about someone's feelings, it causes more harm than good. People begin to question how they should feel or if they should feel.

For many people, sharing their feelings takes courage. They have something to share that is difficult and scary. They need to know that when they share their feelings, you are a safe person to share their feelings with.

If your response to them sharing their feelings is jokes and laughter, they will hesitate to share with you again or with anyone else. It also causes damage to their emotions and your relationship.

When someone is talking to you about how they feel, just listen. Validate how they feel whether you agree or understand or not. Try to understand and put yourself in their shoes. Try to understand why they feel the way they do.

God wants us to have compassion and understanding for others when they are struggling and hurting. This includes children. Children are just learning how to handle their emotions. Help them learn to regulate their feelings by listening to them when they are upset instead of instantly being upset with them or joking.

Be an emotionally safe person for children to talk to. We all need someone who we regard as safe to talk to about how we feel. Those who are hurting need to know who is safe for them.

Reassure the person who is struggling that you are a safe person and they are in a safe space to share their feelings. If you need to, ask questions to clarify feelings or what is happening that is upsetting the person to whom you are listening.

Maybe events that happened to you in life are a way for you to help someone who is going through something similar. Take time to truly listen to people.

Helping kids to thrive, not just survive, after trauma means listening to feelings and the things that happened to them. We all have feelings. We all have issues in life. Help those around you deal with the hurt and pain to be able to move forward in life. There are no jokes needed—just a listening heart.

Being Bounced Around

We have all played with those little bouncy balls from vending machines or jacks sets. If you bounce them just right, they can fling all over the room. They can hit every wall and corner. They are fun to play and "experiment" with.

Playing with a rubber ball is one thing. It is a toy. There is a different kind of bouncing around that is not as much fun—when kids bounce around between parents' homes or bounce around from living situation to living situation.

Kids need constancy and to feel safe in their environment. They need to know what they can expect. Kids need limits and boundaries. This is how they thrive. When a child has to go between homes, back and forth between living situations, they struggle.

They struggle with adjustments. They have a hard time feeling safe many times. They may act out. They have meltdowns for no apparent reason. It is very hard on a child to adjust. Many times, there are different rules and expectations in each home. They may only be there for short periods of time. They may have a hard time if their visits are longer, like a week versus a weekend.

Some children do not want to go back and forth. It causes confusion and places stress on them. They develop attachment issues. They cry and get upset because they miss their other parent.

Then there are times when they visit their other parent, and in that home, the adults may talk in a negative way about the other parent. Please do not do this. I understand it is easy to do sometimes, especially out of frustration. The person you are really hurting is your child. Your child is part of both of you. They love their other parent, even if you do not.

Kids go through so many things when they have to go between homes. Some feel like they really do not have roots planted in one place. Some like one parent over another, but if they voice how they feel, they worry someone's feelings will be hurt.

How can adults make this easier on children? They can provide support and a listening ear. Ask what they do with their other parent. Encourage the relationship with the other parent. Allow them to voice their frustrations to you or a trusted friend or family member. Allow them to bring personal items back and forth between homes.

Helping kids to thrive through trauma is to let them just be kids. Give them time to adjust. Understand their frustrations. Give them grace. Allow them to come back to you and cry, because their time with their other parent was rough or they missed you. Kids need to feel safe voicing their feelings to someone. If not you, then find a trusted child therapist to help. If children are not allowed to voice how they feel, it will become a bigger problem later on.

CHAPTER

4

COPING WITH TRAUMA:

THE GOOD, THE BAD, AND THE UGLY

Substance Abuse and Family Counseling

When someone in the family uses substances, whether it is drugs or alcohol, their substance use affects everyone. The whole family suffers and plays different roles for the substance user. Whether they are enabling, or in denial that there is even a problem, or trying to just get through each day, everyone is affected.

Oftentimes it takes many events to happen before the substance user comes to the point of truly wanting or being forced to get help. It may be their spouse leaving with the children, the children being removed from the home by a child protective services agency, or for some other legal issue, like jail time. Everyone has their own rock-bottom point.

When the substance abuser is a teen, the parents may feel that their child does not have a problem, or the parent also uses so they think this is normal, or they may be in total shock and not sure what to do. The family members may be trying to figure out where and how to get help, not only for the substance user but for the family as a whole.

The bottom line, at this point, is the substance user needs to seek counseling. They may even have it forced on them by the judicial system. In other words, they are mandated by the courts to seek counseling for the addiction. Usually this happens after they have gotten in trouble with the law.

When dealing with substance use, the whole family needs to be involved in the counseling process. There are reasons their family member is using drugs or alcohol, and those reasons affect each member individually as well as the family as a whole. These issues need to be worked out in therapy not only for the substance user but for the individual members of the family.

If it is the case of a parent with substance use problems, the children and spouse are probably very hurt and angry. There are most likely issues of trust, or lack thereof, in the family because the substance user has lied or manipulated other family members. These are all issues that need to be addressed in family counseling. Children need to be able to express what they think and feel to their parents in a safe place.

Part of my caseload is working with the children and teens of substance users. These children are hurt and angry. They know what their parent is doing is not okay, but they are children so they do not know what to do about it. They are stuck. In some cases, because their parent or parents cannot take care of them properly, children are placed in foster care or go live with another family member.

Some children end up with the sober parent and they are trying to figure out what to do next. Again, they know what their parent is doing is not okay, and yet their parent still "chooses" alcohol or drugs over their family or children. Children feel neglected, angry, scared, and frustrated.

The spouse needs to be able to express their feelings about how the substance use has affected the family. Counseling the family as a whole is an important part of restoring the family unit. For some couples, the best thing is marriage counseling to help figure out what to do and how to handle the substance use and other issues. For a couple, marriage counseling to help restore the relationship and help support the substance user is just as important as family counseling.

In the case of teens who use, parents need to take a step back and realize their teen is in serious trouble. The teen needs support and love in order to recover from their substance use issue. Parents need to realize their role in their teen's recovery and what they can do to help their teen. This could be a change in rules or setting consequences; in general, the teen will be held accountable for their actions.

Teens usually have reasons to use, like any substance user. Teens might be trying to cover some kind of hurt or pain in their lives. If this is the case, your teen needs counseling not only for the substance use but also for the hurt and pain in their life. When I counsel teens, I include the parents in the counseling process. I as a therapist can only do so much to help a teen in my office once a week. They need tools they can use at home too. Teens also need parents who will help them when they want to use in order to cope with a stressor.

Many believe the reason teens use is peer pressure. While this is true to a point, teens develop a substance use issue to cover some kind of trauma such as divorce, abuse, low self-esteem, bullying, and so on. Teens want to fit in and pretend that everything is "normal." The job of a counselor is to help them with the underlying issues and hopefully help with the substance use issue as well. The most effective way to do this is to involve the parents and other family members.

While counseling for individual family members is important and needed, counseling for the family as a whole is also needed. The family needs to talk all together about issues and work things out together as a family unit. There may be things the substance user is not even aware happened and need to be worked out or family dynamics that are not healthy that need to change to help the family function better.

The sibling needs to be able to express to their substance user sibling how they feel about their substance use. A parent needs to hear the hurt that was caused by the parent to their child during a drunken fit. A parent needs to hear from their substance-using teen why they use, even if that reason is because their parents got a divorce.

In order for the family to be made whole again, the family as a whole need to talk out issues that cause the substance use. They also need to talk out the issues caused by the substance use, divorce, financial problems, fighting, neglect, hurt feelings, and so on. Until this happens, there will continue to be problems in the family.

The key is finding an appropriate therapist or group of therapists who can work with the individual family members as well as the family as a whole. They can also help the family plug into resources in order to have complete care and recovery for every family member.

Finding a therapist who not only understands substance addiction but also family dynamics is what would work best. As frustrating as it may be to have a family member who abuses substances, still understand your family as a whole needs help and to not be afraid to reach out to get the help that is needed. This is helping kids to thrive, not just survive.

Numbing the Pain

Talking about trauma and how to handle trauma in the lives of the ones we love, including ourselves, comes with a lot of pain and hurt. All anyone wants is the pain to go away, whether it is physical or emotional. Pain is pain.

When talking about emotional pain, there are medications which can help with anxiety and depression if taken properly and prescribed by a doctor. These medications along with therapy are meant to help people handle the anxiety and depression that comes with traumatic life events.

Then there is a whole other set of "medications" which are used to "help" numb the pain. These "medications," or what most therapists refer to as self-medicating, are illegal drugs and alcohol. These drugs are used by many people young and not so young to help numb the pain they feel from life. It is their way of escaping life's problems.

There is one big problem with this ... well, many, really. One problem is the problems are still there. They do not just go away. The pain is still there too. The problems and pain are just being numbed by using substances.

Another problem is using substances creates more problems. No matter the age of someone using, it causes more problems—legal, employment, school, issues at home—and then there is the domino effect. These issues then affect others around the person using.

It affects their families. So many children end up being removed from their parents because of substance use issues in the home. Children who have a parent who uses can be abused or neglected.

People who use substances have a very hard time getting or keeping a job. They have discipline issues at work. They may even be fired from their job.

How to help someone who is trying to numb the pain with substance use is to help them with their pain. They have pain they are too afraid to deal with. They most likely have had some sort of trauma. The pain from the trauma is so deep it is hard to see or deal with.

Helping young people with trauma is something that is key and which may help prevent the start of substance use. Prevention is the biggest way to help with substance use.

Children and youth who have childhood trauma do much better if the issues are addressed while they are young. They learn coping skills that are healthy like anger management and setting boundaries which will help them into adulthood.

Of course, coping skills are also helpful for adults. No

matter one's age, it takes a lot of work and support to be able to overcome trauma and unhealthy coping skills. This is helping kids or adults thrive after trauma, not just survive.

Choosing to Die

Have you had such a bad day or time in your life that you thought of dying? Or just not wanting to be around? Have you ever been in so much pain you would rather die than to continue in pain? Many people would say yes at least in their minds, if not out loud.

We have a very real nationwide problem. People die every day by choosing to take their own life. They complete suicide or at least attempt it. They are in such emotional or physical pain that they just want to end their life. They see no other way out.

Many who have experienced trauma have had these thoughts at least once during their journey of surviving trauma. They have thoughts that life for others would be better if they were not around or that suicide is a way of escaping the trauma.

This is so far from the truth. Many young people, for example, are being so badly bullied that they want to die, or they want to kill the person who is bullying them. Kids are telling other kids to just go and die or that life would be better without them. This is a serious problem with serious consequences.

People who want to die or think suicide is the only way out have become so wounded that they are numb to their emotions. It hurts too badly to talk about it so they do not. Or they have tried to talk about it and no one has listened to them. They have tried reaching out for help and not gotten the help they need.

When we talk about suicide, people worry it will give people the idea to commit suicide. This is so far from the truth. If we talk about suicide, then it allows someone who has been thinking about it to talk about it with you.

Talking about suicide can actually bring to light what is bothering this person. In most cases, they really do not want to die. They just do not see any way out from their pain and hurt. They hurt so badly that they just want the pain to end. They need to know there are other ways to get help and how to get it.

I never take anyone lightly who says they are suicidal or thinking of suicide. We talk about it. We talk openly. We find ways to deal with the hurt and pain instead of dying. We talk about the feelings and the pain they are having and try to do some problem solving. Then we talk further about how to make things better for them.

Victims of trauma have most likely been suicidal at least once. We need to shine a light on the trauma. We need to help them get out of the trauma and move beyond it. Trauma is something that lasts a lifetime if not handled properly.

When helping someone who says they are suicidal, there are things to take into consideration. First, unless you are a medical or mental health professional, you need to help this person seek services. This usually means a trip to the emergency room.

Try not to fall apart. This just makes it worse. They are scared and you falling apart and being scared does not help. Also, do not go the other direction and ignore them. They are reaching out for help. If you cannot help them, then find someone who can.

Just because they say they are suicidal does not always mean they want to die. It means they need help and do not know any other way to get it. When you help someone who has experienced trauma by helping them through being suicidal, you are helping them to not just survive, but to thrive.

Cutting the Pain

We have all had some kind of injury that is so painful that we can hardly move or function. We may have a cast, a bandage, a sling, or stitches to show the wound we have. These wounds are easy to see and determine what happened.

Then we see a different kind of wound. Some people are in so much emotional pain that they harm themselves. I know this sounds strange to some people. Why would someone hurt themselves on purpose?

Self-harm is a growing problem. Teens who self-harm are the ones I see the most. They cut or do some other form of self-harm. They cut because they hurt so much emotionally, and they do not know how to handle it.

People cut or self-harm for a variety of reasons. It could be the trauma they have experienced. It could be feelings they have that they do not know how to handle in a healthy way. No matter the reason, it is cry for help.

People who self-harm need help. They are asking, crying out for help. They feel so numb in their feelings that they cut or self-harm to feel some kind of pain, even if it is physical.

Most of the time, they cut in places not easily seen. They cover up their cuts with long sleeves, bracelets, long pants, or hoodies. They do not want anyone to see their scars because they are embarrassed.

They know what they do is not a solution to their problem; however, they do not know any other solution. They need a professional who knows how to handle someone who cuts or self-harms. They need someone who won't shame them or hurt them further.

When you discover someone you love is cutting or practicing some other form of self-harm, do not shame them. Also, do not panic. Listen to them without judgment. Show concern for them about why they have gone to these measures.

They need professional counseling and mental health services. They need support to deal with what they are feeling. They need someone who will listen to them. Understanding why someone would cut or harm themselves is part of helping them.

If we can understand the why of it, we can better help the person who is cutting themselves. They do not like the idea of cutting. They are scared of their feelings and do not know any healthy ways of handling their feelings.

Helping someone to thrive and not just survive trauma sometimes means dealing with things that are downright scary. If you feel out of your realm or comfort level or just plain overwhelmed, reach out for help. Self-harming behavior is not something to be taken lightly. It is a very serious issue and not something someone outgrows or just stops doing.

Coping with Life

When anyone goes through life, they learn ways to handle the ups and downs. It is easy when life is good and fun. It is easy to go play and deal with the little things that hit us. We can brush those things off and move on.

What about the times when life is not the best? Or just downright awful? How do people, including kids, handle trauma or traumatic events in their lives? I am sure we could list all kinds of unhealthy ways to deal with things. Some of these are just a given, like when kids have meltdowns.

We need to remember what happened to someone to get to the point of stress and turmoil. Part of my job as a therapist is to help children and teens find ways to handle their trauma in a way that is healthy and helpful.

Some suggestions for kids and parents are journaling, being physically active, and being creative. Talk to a trusted person—it could even be the dog, if it helps. I also teach kids and teens how to set boundaries with people, to help keep them safe from further harm. We talk about ways to talk about what happened to them, as the victim, to help them process the trauma.

There are ways to handle trauma and people who hurt them with minimal drama and stress. Setting boundaries is a big one:

- Let your "yes be yes" and your "no be no"
- Don't worry about what others think about your choices
- Stand up for yourself or your child to protect and care for them
- Limit communication with someone because of how they treat you or your child

We as therapists talk about self-care, the ability to take care of yourself so you can handle life better and deal with stress. Self-care is not always sitting on the couch watching endless movies. It is also eating well, exercising, going to the doctor, seeking mental health services, and so much more.

Part of my self-care is spending time with God. I talk to Him and read His word daily. I try my best to hand things over to Him that are stressing me. God can help you with whatever your situation is, including trauma.

When we use unhealthy ways of coping with trauma and stress, it just makes the situation worse and sometimes a lot worse. If you or someone you love is using unhealthy coping tactics, try reaching out to get them help but also set your limits with them too.

Helping kids (or anyone) thrive through trauma is dealing with the problem and coping with it in a healthy way. We sometimes cannot stop bad things from happening, but we can always learn ways to deal with it better.

CHAPTER

5

MOVING BEYOND TRAUMA

Taming the Trauma Monster

When someone uses the word trauma, we automatically think of all these bad things that could have happened to someone we love or to ourselves. Usually, we think of things like abuse, witnessing a horrible event, a death, or some other bad occurrence. Trauma can be one event or many. Trauma can be all kinds of things.

In my experience, for most children who experience trauma, it is usually more than one thing. Usually something big is the trigger, then there are other things that happen as a result. The trauma may be a parent death and that triggers more things that happen, for example, moving to a new house, a parent working more, living with grandparents, or the remaining parent emotionally or mentally "checking out."

Traumatic events can happen at any age. Childhood trauma is hard to handle because the aftereffects can last a lifetime. Some of the signs of trauma are anxiety, nightmares, poor attention span, struggles in school or home, behavior issues (acting out), anger, and the list goes on.

Trauma is not something to just "get over." It leaves scars for years. The wounds can be huge. Imagine having a bullet hole wound and trying to cover it with a Band-aid. It just is not going to fix the problem. Trauma is a big deal.

Helping children and teens through a traumatic event or many events is not easy. It takes a lot of time and patience. There are many factors involved. Then when it seems like they have a handle on their coping skills and trauma, something else sneaks in—the trauma monsters.

The trauma monster is the big, ugly thing that no one wants to deal with. People will avoid it at all costs. The pain is so real, and for many, they think it is better to just sweep it under the rug and pretend it did not happen. There is a problem with this idea—the trauma monster always comes back, most of the time bigger and worse than ever.

The trauma monster is a sneaky thing too. He likes to just sneak up out of nowhere. The trauma monster may hit when a person sees someone who reminds them of their abuser or when a person who was involved in a house fire smells smoke.

When someone is dealing with the trauma, they need to seek professional help. They need someone who has experience in trauma therapy. The trauma monster can be tamed with the proper help. It is hard and scary, but in the end, those trauma wounds heal much better. Taming the trauma monster will take time, but it will be so worth the effort.

Be a Duck

We have been told many different ways and by many different people, including God, to let stuff go that bothers us. Scripture tells us to "cast all our anxieties on Him for He cares for you" (1 Peter 5:7). Notice it does not say some anxieties, but all. I know this is easier said than done especially when there have been some major struggles or traumas in one's life, particularly as a child. It is hard to just drop it and let it go.

God created ducks to swim in water and just let the water roll off their backs. I tell the kids I work with all the time to just let the little things or the things they cannot control roll off their backs. These would include other kids saying mean things, calling them names, teasing, or other irritations that come their way.

This can solve a lot of stress and anxiety in life. Let things go. Having deep hurts and pain for a lifetime is something that is hard to just let roll off your back. But the longer you hang on to that pain, the harder your heart becomes and the harder it is to let it go.

When I counsel my kiddos, I talk to them about being like a duck and letting things roll off their backs—things that do not matter much in the grand scope of life. Does it matter that not everyone likes you? If my kiddos can get in the practice of letting things roll off their back, life becomes less stressful for them. When they understand that they cannot control everything around them, life becomes less stressful.

Usually, kids who have control issues also have had trauma in their lives; one event or many. For some reason, they feel like they have no control in their lives, so they try to find other things to control.

The aftereffects of this can be disastrous. This is when things like anxiety, depression, substance use, anger, poor relationships, and any other negative coping skills come into play later in life. Helping kids and teens see they cannot control everything around them is difficult, but necessary.

If I can teach a kid to be a duck and let things roll off their back and teach them better coping skills to prevent the bad stuff from coming out, then I see that as a success. I even make them quack in my office just so they remember to be a duck.

The Bullet Hole Wound and the Band-Aid

Many people, at one point, have been cut or injured so badly they required a trip to the emergency room and some stitches. Some were even taken by ambulance. The wound was so big, a Band-aid would not stop the bleeding. If they did not get medical treatment, there would have been dire consequences. They could have bled to death given enough time.

This is also true of an emotional trauma. If emotional pain is left uncared for, eventually it will lead to physical pain. It could lead to depression, anxiety, blood pressure issues, and overall physical pain.

Like a deep cut needs to be fixed, so does an emotional one, just in a different way. It may take longer than a trip to the ER, but it will heal given time and the proper treatment. The proper person also needs to help people heal.

Just like a physician stitches up our wound, the Great Physician stitches up our emotional wound. That is the only way we will heal properly. Emotional traumas are a mess. They can lead to all kinds of things that create other messes.

When people seek help with their emotional hurts, it is wise to choose a professional therapist trained in trauma therapy. This person would preferably be a Christian therapist who will hopefully guide and direct people to not only heal emotionally, but mentally too.

I am a Christian therapist. I counsel children. I have been referred to as a "feelings doctor" by one of my clients. I proudly accept this title. I do try my best to help hurting children and their families with the help of God. This is the type of therapist people need to be seeking to help them heal. We are out there—just look.

That emotional wound will take time to heal. It will not happen overnight. Just like a physical trauma, mental and emotional traumas take time too. Those stitches may bust open and need to be re-stitched. Some scary things may have to be stared down to be mended properly.

God will be there every step of the way. He will listen, help, and protect—just ask. God is there waiting.

Trying to use other methods of healing like self-medicating with illegal drugs or alcohol will not make the problems go away. All it does is make the problems worse or create more problems.

The process of healing from any trauma, whether physical or mental, is not something that can be rushed. Take time to heal. Go easy. Put yourself in the hands of the Great Physician. He will help heal you in a mighty way if you let Him.

Lego Walls

Kids love Legos. I have a big bin in my office and that is usually the first thing they go for. They want to build and create. They use their imagination to build things. Does this just apply to Legos? Don't we build walls? Do you know a kid who seems to have walls built?

Sometimes kids build walls to protect themselves from hurt and pain and these walls are built out of something much stronger and bigger than Legos. They are built out of hurt, pain, and fear. These walls are built because someone they trusted hurt them badly.

These walls take a while to build and even longer to tear down. They may even take a lifetime. Some people have a wall the size of the Great Wall of China. When people have been hurt or have had trauma, these walls went up for protection, a way to survive life and pain. The reasons for their walls are legitimate. They have been hurt and now they are trying to keep safe.

What they do not realize is that their walls are doing more harm than good, keeping them from people they need in their lives. They need help rebuilding their wall of trust with the people they can trust in their lives.

Some walls need to come down brick by brick. They may be reconstructed many times and taken down many times. Just like playing with Legos, building walls can change. There may be a door of some kind to let a few people in.

When a child lets you past their wall, take it as a compliment. This means they trust you to a degree. They may take a long time to trust you and feel safe with you. Just be patient. They have been hurt before and are scared. Get to know them and their hurts and pain.

Keep your promises. Keep their secrets the best you can for their safety. Reassure them. Those walls will come down, eventually. Try not to get frustrated or take it personally. Try to put yourself in their shoes.

When you are dealing with kids and walls know they want to trust someone—you. They are just scared. Help them ease their fears by being there for them. Take it slow. Understand their hurt and pain. Listen to them. Be someone they can rely on.

Even just sit on the floor with them and play. This helps build a relationship with them. You put yourself on their level. Play a game, play with their toys, play with Legos. Help take down the walls.

Good Grief

After any kind of trauma or traumatic event, there is a time of grief. There are stages of grief everyone goes through, not in any particular order. Sometimes they go back and forth and sometimes they jump around out of order. Sometimes grief can last for days, weeks, or years.

There are good ways of handling grief and not so good ways of handling grief. Grief is the process of dealing with a loss—it could be the loss of a job, a loved one, a relationship, a home, and any other major loss. Traumatic events are a loss.

When someone goes through a divorce, that is a loss. They

are grieving that relationship whether as a child or an adult. There is a mourning process that happens. There are healthy ways of handling this process.

Get enough rest—a person's body will signal it needs rest. Listen and know the limits. When going through grief, one's ability to handle stress is lessened. Try to reduce stress as best as possible.

Set boundaries—express these in the best way possible. Do not worry about what other people think. This is not being selfish. At this time, emotions and mental abilities are all over the place.

Be attentive to needs—eat well and exercise. Do enjoyable things ... for me, it is photography. Talk to trusted friends or family. Talk to God. Read His Word. Do something creative.

Everyone has seasons of grief they go through. It will be okay in the end. Healing is possible. While grieving, it's important to not do self-destructive things like cutting, drinking, drugs, and so on to cover feelings. It is a temporary solution to the problem.

Yes, it hurts to go through the grief process, but it is necessary. It will help the healing process. Yes, there will be a scar. Be patient and allow time to heal.

If you are struggling with trauma or grief issues, know that you are not alone. Sometimes having a support group is helpful or seeking professional services may be needed to help deal with the emotions of trauma.

A loss is a loss. Everyone grieves differently and in different ways. There is no one way to go through grief. It is part of the healing process. Grief does not have a time frame.

Some days will be better than others. Grief is part of life. Going through grief in a good way is part of learning to thrive, not just survive.

I'm Tired of Talking

Some kids I talk to just do not want to talk. They are nervous. They are tired of talking. They are shy. When kids talk about things, I may ask them how they feel about something and they say, "I don't know." They truly may not know especially if it is something that is hard to talk about like trauma.

When kids talk about something that has scared them or caused a major trauma, they may be reluctant to talk about it or they may change the subject. I take this as a cue that they do not want to talk about it. I tread carefully, but I may try to push through their reluctance. I may ask them if they are tired of talking about the trauma.

Keep in mind, when a victim of trauma, whether a child or adult, has to tell and retell their story, it is exhausting. It is not just telling some little story. They are reliving their trauma over and over every time they have to talk about it.

They go through the emotions and events again and again. Some things they simply block out. They honestly do not remember because it is too scary. They are tired of telling their story to so many people. They also worry about who they can trust. They worry if they or someone else will get in trouble.

It takes time for kids or adults who have experienced trauma to be willing to tell their story to someone they trust. When a victim of trauma has to tell their story, let them do it in their own way. They can write it, draw it, or tell it part by part. Let them set the pace. Ask questions only to clarify.

Telling a trauma story is not easy. It takes a lot of bravery in order to do it. When one of my clients finishes telling their trauma story, we talk about how brave they were for telling. I reassure them that their story is safe with me.

Part of recovering from trauma is being able to tell their story and not letting it bother them to do so. This is a hard point to get to, but once they do, it is freeing. It takes time. Do not rush a person telling their story to get them to this point so they can be "better."

Someone's personal trauma is not something from a television show or a movie. It is their life. It is not something to be shared with others through gossiping. Let a person deal with their trauma so they can move on in life. Trauma changes a person for a lifetime. Helping victims of trauma by telling their story is helping them thrive, not just survive.

There is No Place Like Home

Most people have a home to go to. They want their home to be comfortable and a place to relax. Home is where they can be themselves and not worry about the outside world. What happens when someone has two homes? Can someone really have two homes?

Children who go back and forth between their parents' houses feel like they just get bounced around. They feel like they miss out on so much when they are going back and forth. There is usually one parent's house that is more "home" to them than the other.

In many cases, there is not much consistency between homes. Rules and expectations can be different. The people they live with are different. Their room is different. At one home a child may share a room and at another they may have their own room. Bedtime may be different.

All of these things can cause a child major stress. This just adds to the tension and behavior issues at home, no matter which home they are at. It usually takes a child a day or two to readjust to coming and going between homes. There is usually some sort of "acting out" or emotional meltdowns that happen during this process.

Depending on what happens at the other parent's home, the child may have had to "hold in" their emotions, so when they return to the other parent's home, it all comes flooding out.

Some children become clingier when it is time to go to the other parent's home. They may have more meltdowns in the days leading up to going to the other parent's home. After a divorce, there is a time of adjustment to going between homes for children. They need to get used to their new schedules and routines. You cannot rush this process. If you try, it will backfire badly.

Seeking professional help for your child is something that could be very helpful. This person would give your child a neutral person to talk to and share coping skills to better handle the stress of switching homes.

Children need structure and consistency to thrive. When they are switching homes, this becomes a struggle. When parents are attempting to co-parent, they need to keep this in mind. Helping children to have as much consistency as possible will help this situation so much more.

Talk with the other parent and find ways you can be consistent between homes to better help your child. Having a family calendar and marking on it when children come and go from the home also helps, no matter their age. Write it in a special color. This is a visual not only for parents but also for children.

Divorce is hard on everyone. There are ways to help make transitions easier for all involved. Reminding yourself that your child is the most important part of this will help. This will help your child adjust better in a situation that is downright stressful and scary.

Your child deserves both parents. They do better when both parents can still work together even if they are not living under the same roof. This is helping your child to thrive, not just survive, after trauma.

Putting the Puzzle Together

Many people enjoy putting together a large puzzle. They leave it out and work on it over time. They work at it and work at it. Many people have some kind of strategy in how they go about putting the puzzle together. Maybe they put all the edges together first and then work on the inside.

Putting the puzzle pieces of life back together after a trauma is much like putting a puzzle together. It helps if there is a picture of what the puzzle should look like when it is finished. It is harder when there is no picture.

This is what it is like to put a puzzle back together after a trauma. One tries to pick up the pieces and put them together, but they have no idea what life should look like after a major traumatic event happens.

The pieces are not the same. They are all over the place. They may be damaged, torn, or even missing. It will take longer to put a puzzle together that is missing pieces, just like it will take longer to put life back together after a trauma.

Trauma can be very confusing and difficult to deal with. There are many parts to a trauma. One may not even be aware of all the pieces, especially if they were young when the trauma happened.

It may take many years for all the pieces to come together. Even after some time and work, they may still not have all the pieces. There may even be pieces from other puzzles mixed into theirs.

Trauma is not something someone just "gets over." There needs to be time in order to work through it. There needs to be time to heal. Healing needs to happen at their own pace. Working through a trauma is not easy and should not be done alone.

If you, your child, or someone you know is recovering from a trauma, seek support. Seek professional help. Look for others who may have gone through something similar. There is safety in numbers. They will understand what you are going through. You will also realize you are not alone.

Take time to work through your trauma and what you have gone through. It is not a race. It is a journey. Just like trying to work through a thousand-piece puzzle, working through trauma takes time.

Helping kids to thrive and not just survive trauma takes time, effort, and work. Let them work through it the best they can. Offer support and care when you are able.

Walking in Kid's Shoes

Kids walk, run, skip, jump, and hop. They like to be busy. Some days it is really hard to keep up with them. They are all over the place. Adults can feel that they need running shoes just to keep up.

This is also true for kids who have experienced trauma. They have seen and heard things that no child should ever have to deal with. Some children witness all kinds of hurt and pain. Some children experience it firsthand.

Adults try their best to protect children from harm, but there are still things that happen. To help children recover from trauma, adults need to follow in their little steps to be able to know what they are dealing with every day of their young lives.

Adults need to be able to understand what has happened to the best of their ability so they can help to the best of their ability. Many things children do is for protection and survival. Once adults understand that, they can know how to help. They can also know why children do the "crazy" things they do.

Children who have gone without food will eat nonstop for fear of not having food later. They will hoard food so they have it for later. They will act tough in order to survive to cover up their pain. They will push people away to keep from getting hurt.

To help children thrive through trauma, be the adult who understands why they do what they do. Be the person who understands and actually listens to them—their words and actions.

Children may be afraid to cry or show emotion because they have been hurt in the past. They do not feel heard. They have been hit when they cry. They have been told their emotions do not matter.

Be the safe person who will allow them to cry and get angry. Reassure them it is okay to be angry and sad or even happy or excited or proud. Walk with a child through their emotions. When children share their emotions, they are trusting they will be safe to do so.

Children of trauma have experienced more in their short lives than many adults will ever even hear about in their whole lives. Many children have their innocence taken away from them. They feel alone or abandoned.

Do not be afraid to walk with these hurting children. They are children who need love and to feel safe with someone. It is a big deal to have a child trust you. Do not ever take that for granted. Be a trusted adult who can walk with a hurting child, so they can thrive, not just survive, after trauma.

The Triggers of Trauma

Sight, sound, feeling, taste, and smell—people use their five senses to take in the world around them. This includes traumatic events. When people experience something traumatic like a car accident, a death, an abusive relationship, or a divorce, even long after these events have happened, memories still flood their senses.

In those situations, especially in trauma which has happened over a length of time, people develop ways of surviving on a day-to-day, moment-to-moment basis. Many people who are around them probably do not understand why they do those things.

For example, a child who has experienced neglect, abuse, and hunger may hoard food in their room, locker, or desk. They may steal food from classmates because they are hungry. They do this for survival. They may be afraid or embarrassed to ask for help so they just take what they need, hoping no one finds out.

For some people, driving by a particular house or some other physical landmark brings back memories for them. Children may be afraid to go to a certain person's house because of something that happened to them while they were there, like abuse or sexual assault.

Some triggers may never be understood by anyone. Most can be figured out so the victim of the abuse can get the help they need to deal with it appropriately. Many times, it takes keen observation to figure out what triggers someone and why. Some things are easy to figure out.

When helping a child with trauma issues, reassure them that they are understood and you are there to help them—this is the best thing you can do. They need this consistently. They need to know there will always be food for them. They need to know they will always be taken care of and provided for.

You, as the adult, may be the first person in their young lives to be the constant. This process will take a long time, years for many. This will also take patience and understanding when helping a child victim of trauma. Reassurance is the key to this process. Child victims of trauma need to know you can be trusted. You may be the first adult they trust.

Helping a child thrive, not just survive, after trauma is not for the faint of heart. It takes a lot of understanding, patience, and grace. These children are broken and hurt. If we are to truly help them move beyond their trauma, we need to help them understand and process through their triggers. This is the point, if not before, that professional mental health services for children or teens should be found.

Be a Storyteller

Many kids love to hear stories and tell them. They love to know what happens next or try to guess. They also like to share about their day or be creative and make up their own story. Many children share stories easily. They may even love to act it out. This can be so fun and entertaining for both the child and the audience.

Then, there are stories that are not so easy or downright scary to tell. Children are worried that if they tell stories it will bring up negative or scary feelings. Children who have experienced trauma many times have a hard time sharing "their story" of what happened.

There are so many reasons why they feel this way. They may:

- Be too scared

- Have been threatened to not tell
- Feel like if they tell, no one will believe them
- Not be sure how to tell what happened
- Be confused about what happened and how they feel
- Be afraid to tell you as their parent because they have been threatened
- Worry you will be angry

All of these reasons are why it is helpful to have a child therapist for your child to talk to. A therapist who is trained in working with childhood trauma can help your child and you sort out all of these reasons and concerns. A therapist gives your child a safe person to talk to who is neutral and your child feels safe with.

The therapist can help your child be able to tell "their story" of trauma. They can help your child have a voice when they may not feel like they do. Being able to talk about what happened to them is the most valuable thing you can do for a child who has gone through trauma. Yes, you will have to be there and be part of the process for it to be effective.

Many of the children I counsel want their parent in the room for support. Some would rather talk in private so they can tell me how they feel without worrying about what their parent thinks. Your child needs to know you are part of their support system.

Children who have experienced trauma have gone through so much. They have a hard time being able to sort it out. They may be more likely to just not talk about it. The longer this going on, the worse it gets. Trauma needs to be talked about and dealt with in order to heal.

Helping your child process through their trauma is key in helping them to grow beyond it and handle the scary things in life. If your child tries to bury the problem or pretend it did not happen, it just makes the trauma or wound worse.

Helping kids to thrive, not just survive, after trauma means being able to talk or tell their story to a trusted person. It means being able to not be afraid to voice how they are feeling no matter what has happened. Making yourself approachable and available to children, whether they have experienced trauma or not, is what we all as adults need to do. This is helping kids thrive, not just survive trauma and life.

Stitching Emotional Wounds

Big hurt requires big care. There is a big wound that is wide open and oozing pain and hurt. The pain is so raw but one does not want to even bring it up for fear of falling apart. Stitching an emotional wound is not an easy process. It is downright painful.

Emotional wounds, like physical wounds, take time to heal. It takes time to rebuild strength. Just like a physical injury, emotional hurts take time to heal ... maybe even years.

The problem with emotional wounds is they are harder to see. On the outside, physical appearance looks all healthy and well. On the inside, hurt and pain are just right under the surface.

When someone is trying to recover from emotional pain, it is one of the hardest things a person can do in their lifetime, no matter their age. When someone has trauma on top of trauma, the pain and healing take even longer.

Coming alongside a hurt person is a most valuable thing that can be done. When we help a child or adult with their trauma and help them in the recovery process to heal, this is the most helpful thing we can do. It is messy. It is hard. You will struggle and so will they. They will want to give up. You may want to give up.

The stitching process is not a fast process. It takes time and care. If we are going to help kids or anyone thrive and not just survive trauma, we need to be kind and compassionate to them. Offer support and guidance, not judgment and rude comments.

Helping kids to thrive through trauma means understanding they are fighting battles most of us will never understand. They are fighting invisible enemies. Some days they feel like they are winning. Other days they feel like they are falling flat on their face.

We help them get back up and march forward. Keep going, keep pushing, keep working toward their goals. Stitching emotional wounds is a lot of work and time.

The wounds of trauma will always be there. They never really go away. But, helping them heal so kids can move on and function is a key part in the healing process.

Will they need help from time to time as they go forward in life? Of course. Will they need reassurance from time to time? Yes. But helping them become productive adults and be able to move on from the hurt is helping kids to thrive, not just survive trauma.

CHAPTER

6

GOD HEALS THE HURT

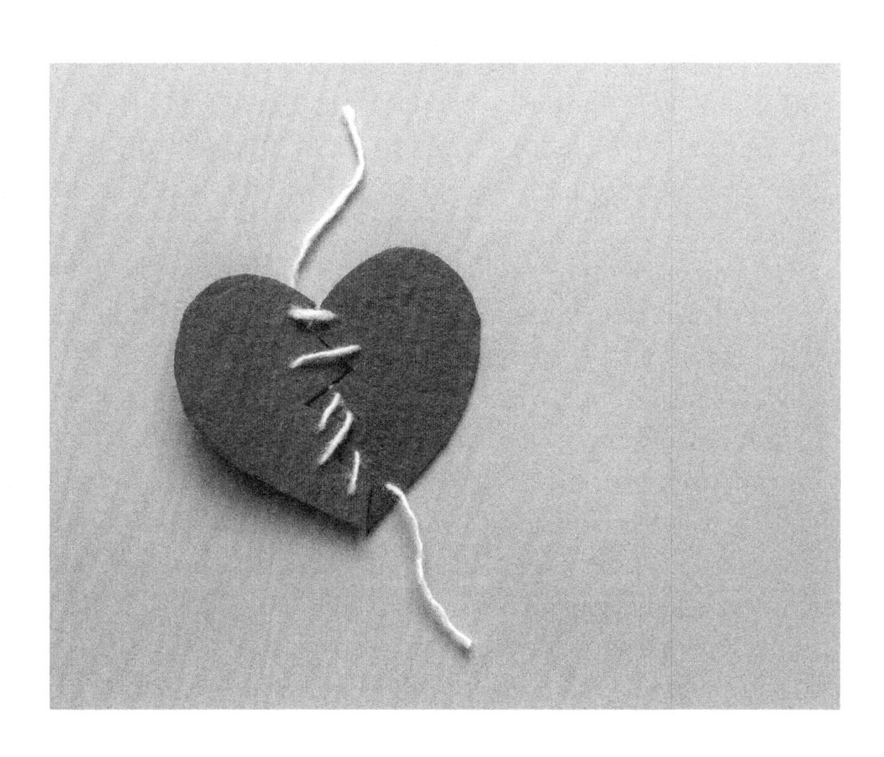

Close to the Brokenhearted

God knows when we are sad. He knows when we are in pain both mentally and physically. He is close to the brokenhearted. He is with us in our darkest times. God knows when we are scared. He gets angry at those who hurt us. He is angry with those who harm any of His children.

God knows when one of His children is hurting. We are all His children no matter our earthly age. He wants to protect us from harm. Many people question why God lets bad things happen. Bad things happen because God created us to have free will. He also knows there is evil and sin in the world too.

This is hard for us to understand or accept, especially when we or someone we are close to is hurting or they have had bad things happen to them. God does not make mistakes. He knows what is happening in our lives. Nothing surprises Him. He knows there is pain and sin in the world.

This is why He sent His one and only Son to save us from our sin. God gave us hope through Jesus. God also gives us hope to know He will protect us from those who intend to do harm or hurt us.

God knows the hurt and pain felt by those who have gone through trauma experience. He understands and is just a prayer away to help us deal with the hurt we have endured. He is a loving Father who wants nothing but the best for His children. He gets upset and angry when His children are hurt by sin.

God is there to help us with our pains and hurts. He is there to guide us and help us heal from pain. He knows our pain and what needs to happen to be healed from our pain. He will help us forgive those who have hurt us.

The only One who can help heal us is God. He is the One

who our abuser or the person who hurt us will have to answer to. God is the One who will punish them for their sins against us. That is God's job, not ours.

Our job is to obey Him and let Him heal us from the traumas we have endured. God will protect us, like any loving Father would His children, except He is better than our earthly father, because He is God.

God uses those hurtful or traumatic experiences to help us grow in trusting Him. He knows how to fix the hurt in our lives if we let Him. We need to trust in Him and His ability to heal the hurt we have to help us to thrive, not just survive.

Help! I Hurt!

Many parents have heard their children cry out in pain. They want to rush to their side and help them. Whether it is a small bump or bruise or a major hurt, all a parent wants to do is take care of their child. They want to make the pain go away. It is hard as a parent to watch your child be in pain and not be able to fix it.

I hear this from so many parents of my clients. Their child is hurting emotionally or mentally and parents feel helpless. Their child got their feelings hurt by a friend. They are being picked on at school. A parent just wants to fix it.

This is so true for trauma too. When something traumatic happens to a child, parents and caregivers, myself included, want to fix it. How do we fix this kind of pain?

The pain of trauma runs deep. It is a big pain. It is something that does not just go away. The trauma needs to be dealt with. The pain is just so bad their parents and caregivers are just as frustrated as the child. It is even worse when the trauma is caused by one or both of the parents or another close adult.

The child trusted this adult and got hurt. This is hard for children to understand. It is often hard for adults to understand, too. When we talk about a loving Heavenly Father, many kids have a hard time understanding because of the hurt they have gone through.

Seeking professional help for your child who is experiencing trauma is key. Finding a professional child therapist who can help your child, and you as their caregiver, is so important.

Just as important, if not more important, is asking for healing and help from God. He is our Heavenly Father who heals all our hurts and pains if we let Him. Many times in scripture, all people did was cry out to God, "Help me Lord!" And God was there.

We usually do this when we have tried everything else. Why do we not try this from the beginning? God knows our pain. He feels it. He hurts when we hurt. We are His children. Just like earthly parents want to help their hurting children, God is there too, even when it does not seem like anyone else is.

God wants us to come to Him when we need Him. He wants us to trust Him. It may be hard for you to trust Him because your pain is so big. There is no pain too big for God to heal.

When helping children, there are many times in my career that I pray for clients. I pray for their situations. I pray for God to intervene. I pray for God to protect my clients from further harm.

When we ask for help from God or anyone else, we need to set aside our pride of "I can do this by myself." God created us to help each other. He created us for relationships. Sometimes, those relationships get messy. It is better to ask for help so we can do more than just survive, but we can thrive.

Tears Heal

When we are sad or upset, many times we try to hide how we really feel. We do not want to show our true feelings and be vulnerable to others. We want to show we can handle things.

When someone has experienced trauma, they tend to hide how they feel. They do this for a variety of reasons. They are trying to protect themselves from further hurt. They do not trust others with how they feel.

No matter the reason, bottling up their feelings is not helpful. Their emotions still come out, just not in healthy ways. It comes out as anger or behavioral issues. No matter how much they try to hide their feelings, it comes out.

When we are sad or upset, it is okay to let the tears flow. It is okay to cry. Some people hold back, because they are afraid if they start crying, they will not be able to stop. Sometimes, just having a good cry helps.

It is okay to shed tears and cry when we need to. God wired us with feelings. Even Jesus cried. He cried when His friend died. Jesus was sad. It is okay to be sad too. We are human. We have emotions that need to be expressed.

There are times in life that are just sad. Crying helps us feel. It is a way for us to heal. We are able to feel our true feelings and let them out.

It may be necessary to cry alone. It may be necessary to find someone you trust to cry with. Either way, it is okay to cry. There are times in life that are just hard. It is okay to express your feelings. It is okay to talk about your feelings with a trusted person.

Finding a safe person and a safe space to do so is helpful. Finding someone who will listen to you and how you feel without judgment is also important. Your feelings are valid and need to be listened to with the proper respect.

An important part of healing from emotional pain is to allow yourself to heal. If part of that healing involves crying, then that is okay. Do not be ashamed to let yourself cry and express your feelings in a healthy way.

God made us to have feelings and to be able to express them. Finding a healthy, safe way to share and express yourself is a key part of healing from trauma. Let your tears flow. God will catch them and keep you safe.

Just Drop It

Have you ever tried to carry in all the plastic grocery bags from the car at once? You get yourself in the door and you are about to drop it all. We often do this in other parts of our lives as well. We try to carry too many things.

What about mentally? Do you try to carry too many things? Do your kids? We carry around our emotional baggage because we do not know what to do with it. Kids carry around theirs too. Like adults, they do not know what to do with it.

When we carry around so much baggage, we do not realize we can put it down. We can make the choice to put it down. We carry around bags with hurt and pain, feeling lost or unwanted.

We carry around our life problems like we carry around our gym bag. It is full of stinky, gross, sweaty stuff. We do not want to carry it because it is annoying, hard to hold on to, or just plain too heavy.

We carry these bags into relationships, into our jobs, school, home life, friendships, and in our day-to-day activities. We are tired and worn out from carrying them. But, where do we put them down?

The trick is to put them down and not pick them back up. We put down our nasty, stinky baggage at the foot of the cross with Jesus. We let Him unpack our nasty bags. We let Him clean them up.

There is so much to unpack, and we cannot do it alone. We need help from others around us whom we trust. We also need help from God. He is the one who can help us the most. God knows us and our situation better than anyone else. He knows our pain and hurt. He will take care of it. We can trust Him.

Once we are able to set down our bags, we will feel so free in our lives. We will not have these heavy bags weighing us down. It frees us up to help others and to live life.

Carrying around the baggage from trauma and hurt may as well be a big stone tied to you. It can drown us. It can sink us. It makes life so much harder when we carry it around. Give yourself permission to set down your baggage of hurt and pain.

Unloading the bags for trauma is not easy. Just when you think you have set it down, it seems to be back in your hands. It most likely will take several times of setting down the bags before you are able to do it for good. Keep trying until you succeed. Having supports like a trusted therapist will help you in this process.

Setting down your baggage will help you move on in life. It will help you to thrive, not just survive, after trauma.

Facing the Trauma Giant

We talk about how scary trauma is, what it is, and what it does to a person. Trauma has lifelong effects. Trauma seems like this giant that is always there.

How do we get rid of this giant? We take it out. We battle and fight until it is gone. We get the help we need. We face the scary things involved in trauma. Do not give up. It will get better.

Imagine you are in a battle and it is you versus the giant. You use every weapon you have at your disposal. You learn new coping skills through therapy.

Learn to set boundaries. Boundaries are a powerful weapon and tell people what you will and will not tolerate from them. Boundaries also let your "yes be yes" and your "no be no." Setting healthy boundaries is a major weapon when battling trauma and toxic relationships.

Talk about the feelings attached to the trauma. Reach out for help when you feel yourself slipping into old patterns or feeling discouraged. Another key weapon you also have at your disposal is God. God is there to fight for you.

God is our protector. He is there as our comforter. He will guide you and help you with whatever battle you face. When battling trauma, use whatever you can to stand your ground. God does not want us to hurt or be in pain. He wants us to have healing from our scars.

Satan will try to fight us and use our trauma and the effects of trauma to take us out. He wants us to lose this battle. He wants us to live in misery, hurt, and pain. He wants us to feel trapped and stuck. It is our job to acknowledge when this has happened and reach out to God for His help and protection.

Fighting the giant of trauma is a daily event for many people. It takes a long time to be able to come out the other side and be able to function. Things trigger trauma and sometimes are totally blindsiding. Learning what your triggers are in trauma is a key part of fighting the giant of trauma.

Trauma can be defeated using the right weapons and the right strategies. Using our weapons and fighting trauma head-on is the best way. When we try to hide trauma, it does not usually work so well. It works about as well as hiding a giant in your living room. Facing trauma is hard and scary. But, with the right help, including help from God, the trauma giant can be defeated. This is helping to thrive through trauma, not just survive.

God Wins!

Bad stuff happens to good people ... innocent people ... children and babies. Bad stuff just happens. Trauma is not the victim's fault. It is something that happens to you. You as the victim did not cause it. You were the one who got hurt. No matter what anyone says to you, you did not cause the bad thing to happen.

You did not ask to be hurt by anyone, physically, mentally, emotionally, or spiritually. No one asks to be hurt. The reason bad stuff happens is because sin came into the world. Evil is in the world. Bad things happen that we have no control over. God is there always, even in the bad and ugly.

He is there in it all. When God created mankind, He created us to have free will—the ability to make choices. We can choose to make good decisions or poor decisions. This is how we ended up with sin in the world. We can choose to follow God and try to obey Him. Or we can choose to not follow God and make poor or bad choices.

There are consequences to every choice that is made, whether positive or negative. Unfortunately, those choices affect not just the person who makes the choice but also the one who is the victim of the choice.

Many people who have gone through trauma in their lives blame God. They think God is there to swoop in and stop the bad stuff. He can to a certain point, but there is still evil in the world. We live in a broken world where sin reigns.

What we can trust is, if we trust God, He will do the healing of the trauma and pain in life. He will help us to move beyond the pain and hurt that happened so we can be made whole again. Life is full of hurt, disappointment, and scary stuff. God is there in and through all of it.

Your trauma is not the result of your sin or wrong doing but of someone else's choice. Working through the pain and allowing God to heal you from the inside out will restore you to who God wants you to be.

What we need to understand is bad things, or sins, happen. We can try to protect ourselves and ask for God's protection. People go against God's will and plan all the time. Satan is alive and well. He uses people to hurt and do harm to others who are innocent and do not deserve to be hurt.

Part of learning how to thrive and not just survive trauma is to understand that trauma is not your fault. It also is not something you did. Sin and evil in the world are what caused it. We live in a world full of sin and poor choices. Being able to weave your way through all of this leads to understanding that God does win the war.

Trauma Scars

We all have scars on our bodies. We got stitches or hurt ourselves probably from a very young age. We had a wound that needed medical treatment so it would heal. My first scars, yes plural, I received just after being born. I had open heart surgery at just ten days old. After I was born, I was taken to Ann Arbor, Michigan, to the University of Michigan Hospital.

I had open heart surgery to correct a birth defect. I spent

the first seven months of my life shuffling between the U of M Hospital and my local hospital. From then on, I was taken to the doctors every year for a follow-up, to make sure my heart was doing well and healing.

Some children need a different kind of heart doctor. They need someone who can help heal their hurting heart from trauma. They have been hurt so badly emotionally that they have scars written all over their emotions. Many times, these children have a hard time functioning day to day, moment to moment.

Their symptoms may include outbursts, crying, anxiety, depression, and meltdowns. All of these things are signs of trauma. If left untreated, trauma can leave really big scars. Helping a child to heal from their trauma scars is what my job includes.

Some trauma scars are big like heart surgery, some are small like a couple of stitches. But, if left untreated, they can grow into something bigger, get infected, and cause more problems later in life. If they are treated at a young age, a lot of things could potentially be avoided.

I help children learn to handle their trauma and heal from it. The person who is a way better mental health healer than me is God. Everyone needs God in their lives to help them heal from the hurts and pain this life gives out.

Just like when we fall and get hurt, when life knocks us down, we need to take the time to heal. If we do not heal properly, those scars will hurt and bother us for the rest of our lives. We need to take time to take care of ourselves. Children also need time and understanding to heal.

Children who have experienced trauma have some really big wounds and really big scars. It is our job as supportive adults to help them heal those wounds and treat their emotional wounds like we would their physical wounds—with care and compassion. This is how we help children to thrive and not just survive trauma.

Talk to the Mighty Counselor

Many of us have come to points in our lives where we need to have someone to talk to, but everyone around us seems busy or unavailable. Everyone, that is, except God. He is our counselor who is always around, always available, 24/7, 365 days a year. We can talk to Him no matter where we are in our day.

When we feel alone, scared, or worried, God is there to hear us. The cool thing is, He knows us better than anyone. He knows our thoughts and feelings better than anyone, including ourselves.

When we have good stuff or bad stuff, God is there. He will give us direction. He will give us protection. He will help keep us safe. All we need to do is ask. When we are hurting, He is hurting. When we weep, He weeps.

When people, including children, have gone through a traumatic event, it is important to seek help. It is important to use all available resources. This includes reaching out to God and His church. Seeking wise counsel and Christian fellowship is vital to recovering from trauma. God designed us to be in fellowship with other Christians.

When kids are afraid to go to sleep because they are having nightmares, I encourage them to talk to God. God hears kid prayers too. He wants us all to come to Him with childlike faith.

When we as adults cannot sleep, talk to God. He does not care if you fall asleep midsentence. When we start talking to God about our problems, whether they are large or small, and give them to Him, He can take it from there. Trusting God with our problems is simple and hard all at once, especially when we have been hurt.

We want to be in control. In reality, we are not in control—God is. Being able to pray your way through your day helps in so many ways. It helps relieve anxiety, tension, stress, depression, and gives you direction as well. Some days dealing with hurt and pain are better than others.

Helping anyone to thrive and not just survive after trauma is something that God needs to be a large part of. Prayer and strength from God helps us deal with any life problem we are facing. There are usually many questions that we would like to ask God—"Why did the trauma happen?" or "Why didn't God protect us from harm?" Those are hard questions to answer.

These questions need to be answered through faith and trusting God, that He will work every bad thing out for the good. He knows we hurt. He wants to help us heal from that hurt. The hardest part is letting Him.

Helping anyone thrive and not just survive trauma is pointing them to God and other Christians God places in their path, to help them heal from the pain they have gone through.

Having Justice

One of the hardest things for people who have gone through trauma is feeling like they have had justice or payback for what was done to them. They need to feel that the person who hurt them got a good enough punishment. But some people, no matter what they did, always seem to escape punishment. They never really seem to suffer.

While the justice system never seems to really do justice to people, God does. We may never really see it with our own eyes, but God will do the judging, whether here on earth or in the next life. God is the ultimate judge.

We hope and pray in this life that the person who harmed us or someone we love gets what is coming to them, especially when it comes to a violent crime. We want them to hurt like we hurt.

We want the people who have harmed or scared our children to never see the light of day. We want them to not be able to be free or to be able to hurt another person ever again. We pray and ask God for this. We ask for protection and safety for all who come in contact with this person; that there will not be any more victims.

God never promised us life would be free from pain or problems. He did, however, promise us He will be with us no matter what. Part of what keeps us in pain and hurt is not being able to forgive the person who hurt us.

Lack of forgiveness is what keeps us bound to that person. We are the ones who end up stuck and in pain. When we forgive and let God judge, we are setting ourselves free. This is a very hard step to take, however.

When we forgive, we let go of the pain that keeps us trapped. When we forgive, we do not have to forget what happened. Have the strength to let it go. This will probably have to happen many times for it to finally stick and feel the weight of it off your shoulders.

Forgiveness is not for the person who hurt you. It is for you. It lets you be able to move on in your life and the life of your child. It is hard when the hurt is personal and runs deep. As a parent, you want to protect your children and keep them safe from harm.

Know that no matter how much you as a parent love your child, God loves them even more. He also loves you and knows the hurt you have. Let God be the judge. It is a whole lot less stressful.

Having a Really Good Doctor

When we are sick or our children are sick, we go to the doctor for help and healing. We trust our doctor with the most important thing—our lives or the lives of our loved ones. Doctors have the power to heal us and help us be well. In order to do this, we need to be able to put our trust in doctors. We need to feel comfortable with them.

When we are hurting emotionally and mentally, who do we turn to? Some of us find a really good therapist, one who we trust and can help us sort out our pain and hurt. We trust them with some of the worst things that have ever happened to us in our lives. We trust them with our trauma. We build a relationship with them. This also applies to finding the right therapist for your child as well.

Then there is the Great Physician. He is our Heavenly Father. He loves us even at our lowest points in life. He can reach in and heal our hurts and pains. We need to be willing to trust Him to do so. He has the power to do so. He has the power to help us make it through our hurts and trauma.

God wants us to be happy and healthy, more than anyone. After all, He created us. He wants what is best for us. He wants us to trust Him with our lives, including the parts that hurt and we struggle with.

God wants us to give Him all the pain and hurt we have been through. He wants to take care of it for us. We just need to let Him. This is where trust comes in.

There will be times when the healing process will take longer and be painful, but God is there through it all. He is there to do the healing. He knows our hurts and pain before we even tell Him want is happening. We need to let Him have control in our lives.

Talk to God about your hurt and pain. Tell Him how you feel. Tell Him how angry or scared you are. Pray for protection in your life.

When seeking treatment or help for yourself or your child who has experienced trauma, remember God is always there, even when your therapist is not. Make sure the therapist you go to has the same spiritual beliefs you do. God will direct you to the right person to help you in your time of crisis and need.

Trusting God is another way to help kids to thrive, not just survive, after trauma. Let Him help the healing. You could not ask for a better physician.

The Light at the End of Your Tunnel

When someone, no matter their age, has suffered a trauma, the healing process seems to be never-ending. In many cases it is. The trauma people suffer can last a lifetime, especially if they have had multiple traumas.

Trauma is such an involved and complicated thing. There is no surefire "cure" for trauma. The trauma is there and it is hard work that may last for years in order to feel a "normal" that is healthy.

In many cases, you feel so many emotions. The trauma seems dark and scary. There is no way to get away from it. You may try to run and hide, but it is still there. It is best to face it head-on.

The tunnel seems long and never-ending. In some places it feels so dark that you cannot see the next step ahead of you. Trauma is hurtful. There are so many things that happen as a result of trauma; there are so many changes in your life that you do not know which end is up. You feel like your life is on a roller coaster, and you just want to get off.

There is a light at the end. The hurt and pain become livable or come to an end at some point. There is a light at the end of your tunnel of trauma. That light is Jesus. He is the one who gives you hope.

Jesus gives you hope in your pain. He gives you the light to see what is next. He gives you the strength you need to take the next dark and scary step. He is your protector. He knows the pain you have gone through. He knows you are scared. He is there.

He wants nothing more than to help you heal. He is the ultimate healer and physician. The light at the end of your tunnel is Him. He is also there with you in the tunnel. He is with you every step of the way.

Talk to Him about your pain and hurt. He will understand when no one else can. Talk to Him when life is scary. Talk to Him when you have no one else to talk to. Jesus will give you the strength you need day to day, moment to moment. He will even give you the strength you need to forgive the person who hurt you.

Part of healing is forgiving. The forgiving is not for the person who hurt you—it is for you. It is for you to be able to move on and thrive. Trauma is so painful; just thinking about talking about the person who caused you harm is difficult. You will be able to do this with the help of God. God is there all the time. He knows your heart. He knows your pain.

We have all had hurts and pain in our lives. Some of it is our own doing, some of it is not. We need to forgive ourselves for the things we have done to ourselves and the mistakes we have made.

We also need to forgive those who have hurt us. They may never ask for forgiveness. That does not matter. It makes it harder because we wish they would acknowledge the pain they have caused, but it may not happen that way.

Part of healing and moving on in life is to forgive. Whether that is yourself or someone else, God is there to help you through this process if you let Him. You may have to forgive every day, every moment. It will happen when you least expect it. You will be able to move on from the pain to not only survive, but to thrive.

CHAPTER

7

REBUILDING YOUR LIFE

Hold on … Wait for Me!

When kids are little, they are always trying to keep up with the "big" kids. They run after them yelling, "Wait for me!" They chase after what they want and what they think is important. They want to feel included.

When a child has experienced trauma, in many cases, they need to play catch-up in one or more areas of life. They could need help with catching up on school, emotion regulation, trusting others, building relationships, and so on.

Many times, when a child experiences a trauma or more than one trauma, they stop for a bit. They stay in one place. So, while they are staying still, their peers who have not experienced trauma are moving on by. In the process of recovering from the trauma they have experienced, they will need help and patience to be able to catch up to where they should be developmentally.

It is the job of professionals and caregivers to help these children move beyond the trauma. These children could be fighting the adults who told them they could not do something. They may be fighting their inner voices that say they are stupid or cannot do something. We need to help them get rid of that inner voice, so they cannot only survive, but thrive.

They may need extra help with schoolwork to help them get caught up. They may need help mentally and emotionally with their inner voices that tell them they cannot do something. They need reassurance to rebuild their self confidence in order to be able to push beyond those negative influences in their lives.

Sit down with this child and help them with homework. Get them a tutor. Encourage them to ask for help when they need it. Teach them who to go to for help when they need it.

Encourage them to read—I give books to kids from garage sales and book sales. We make games to make learning fun. Make learning an everyday fun thing to do.

Advocate for them. Stand up for them. Tell their teachers, counselors, and others what kinds of help you believe your child needs. Ask your child what they need help with. You may feel like you are fighting an uphill battle, but you will get there eventually.

Children cannot only survive trauma but thrive in spite of it. They can grow beyond the things that have hurt them to be responsible, intelligent, caring people. They just need some backup and a cheering section to help along the way.

Going, Going, Gone!

Every parent thinks their children grow up too fast. Time just flies when you are raising children. For some children, this is so true. For some children, they have to learn to take care of themselves or others at a young age. The reason? Trauma.

These children are growing up in chaos. They are growing up in homes where they are not able to be children for one reason or another. Some of these reasons could be domestic violence, divorce, or a parent with an addiction or mental illness. The reasons are endless in many cases.

These children are growing up in homes where they may be left alone or unsupervised for long periods of time. They are forced to figure out how to survive because there is not an adult who is caring for them regularly. This is neglect.

I know of children who at a very young age were caring for their younger siblings. They were doing things like finding food to eat, changing diapers, and cleaning up after their siblings, all while their parent was passed out on the couch from being hungover or high.

This becomes a matter of survival for many children with similar stories. They struggle day to day. They barely make it to school. They may even miss school to care for their younger siblings or their parent. This is not the job of children.

The job of a child is to be a child. Let them play, run, play games, have fun. Kids need to be kids. It is not their job to care for the adults. If this is going on, this is a big red flag. Something needs to be done.

It is the job of adults to care for children. It is the job of parents to care for siblings. Yes, having older siblings help with younger siblings sometimes is okay. But, to have to care for younger siblings all the time is not okay. This is neglect. Neglect is a form of abuse. Neglect is trauma.

Leaving your child alone so you can party is not okay either. Your child is more important than getting high. Your child does not deserve this lifestyle—no one does. This is what causes anger and trust issues for children.

This also causes children to worry about what would happen to them if something happened to their parent. Kids see what you do. They see you getting high or drunk. No matter how well you think you hide it, they see it.

When a child is forced to grow up too fast, they struggle with trusting adults. They also try to find other adults to care for them because the ones they have are not doing their job. They may go to grandparents or aunts and uncles or teachers for guidance and care.

In many cases, children are removed and placed in the care of another adult. If you are caring for children with this trauma in their past, let them be kids.

Sign them up for baseball. Let them play. Let them have friends. They need to be kids. Childhood is short enough. Do not make it shorter by making kids grow up faster than they need to.

Keeping Kids Safe

The biggest job of any parent or caregiver of a child is to keep their child safe. They do all they can to keep bad things from happening to their child. They put people in the lives of their child to help them stay safe or talk to when things are not okay.

Schools practice drills to make sure kids know what to do to be safe. They do lockdowns. They do fire and tornado drills. Keeping children safe takes planning.

Part of keeping your child safe is to have a plan—it can be simple or complex, depending on your family situation. When kids feel unsafe, they need reassurance to know things are okay, and they are safe. Also, they need to know who to go to when they need help.

This is a bit of a challenge when children have experienced trauma. Their safety has been taken away. The people they thought they could trust do not exist. Children who have experienced trauma have a very hard time trusting anyone, even into adulthood.

Some things you can do to help keep your child safe are not putting their name on the outside of their clothes or backpack and helping them memorize important phone numbers. Teach them who is not safe, even if it is a parent or grandparent.

Having a plan is the key. Helping kids to have a plan to keep safe helps give them some of the control they feel they have lost. Explaining to kids why someone is not safe, without saying mean or scary things, may be needed. For example, you can say, "It isn't safe to be with daddy right now because he is hurting mommy." Kids understand this because most likely they have witnessed it.

Kids need extra help and reassurance in their lives, some more than others. They need to know they will be protected and kept safe to the best of your ability. Kids who have experienced trauma need to know who they can trust.

Involve your child in your safety plan. Make sure your child's school is aware. Write it down for their teacher. Make sure the school knows who can and cannot pick up your child. Do the same with day care, church, or other activities your child participates in.

Talk to the adults in your safety plan and also explain to them what you need. Kids need to know who they can trust and who you trust with them. Explain to your child what to do if they see someone you feel is unsafe in public.

Hopefully, as time goes on, you will not need all of these safety plans and measures. Keep them in place for as long as you need and beyond. One of the biggest hurdles for kids of trauma to overcome is mistrust and feeling unsafe. You may feel like you are overdoing it a bit, but it is better to be safe than sorry.

Helping kids to feel safe again is a big issue when dealing with trauma and it may take a lot of time. Like anything else with trauma, it also takes patience, understanding, and love. This is helping kids to thrive through trauma, not just survive.

TLC and Trauma

Kids who have gone through trauma are sometimes not the easiest to help or love. They have so many walls and ways of protecting themselves that they may seem like they are angry all the time. Yes, they are angry. They have reason to be angry. They are angry at life. They feel like they got a bad hand dealt to them.

Sometimes we adults look at them and just want to tell them to stop. Don't do this. Children act out because they do not know what else to do. The problem with this tactic is it backfires. They will pull away more. They will close in more. They are acting out to get attention they are lacking from other sources.

Instead, we need to show some tender loving care (TLC). These kids need to be shown patience, love, and support. They need someone who will take their time and help them or listen to them. They just need to be shown what true love and compassion is. They need to be shown grace and forgiveness.

These children need someone who will take their time and correct their behavior in a loving way, not by yelling and hurting them. They are terrified someone else is going to hurt them either physically or mentally.

Many times, when you ask a child who has had trauma why they behave in a certain manner, they do not know why. They honestly do not know. They have learned this behavior as a way of survival. For example, they may have hidden making a mess because other times they got hit when they made a mess.

They need to be taught new ways of coping with life. They need reassurance that their basic needs will be met. They need to be reassured they will not be harmed even if they mess up. They need to be able to rebuild trust in others.

This will take some time, but it can be done. It takes patience and love. Show them what their new "normal" looks like. Some kids will push their limits with you. They do this to see if you will keep your word. They do this to see if you will reject them like all the other adults have done.

You as the adult need to hold your line, to show these hurting children they are loved. They will come to a point when they will trust you. It takes time as they learn to trust you little by little. I tell the kids I work with that I do not expect them to come in my office and trust me right away. I know that it takes time, especially if there is trauma and pain involved.

Kids need to be able to trust adults who are worthy of trust. For many kids, this is hard because of the trauma they have gone through. We do not know what a kid is carrying around with them. We need to earn the trust of these hurting children. They need to feel safe with us.

We need to show love and care to these hurting children. That is the only way they will be able to move beyond their pain and hurt, to a life where they can thrive and not just survive.

The Secrets of Trauma

Children have a hard time keeping secrets, especially fun ones. They want to tell secrets about things like birthday gifts and surprise parties. Children like surprises and fun games.

But when a child is being abused, they are told by the abuser to keep it a secret. They may be bribed with gifts or money or special treatment. They may be told the abuse is a game and it is something special between the abuser and the child. They may be threatened to keep quiet or someone they love will be in trouble or get hurt.

Eventually, these secrets come out. They are accidently told or the child cannot keep the secret anymore. They are scared they will be in trouble or get hurt or taken away from their abuser.

When I work with a child who has been told to keep secrets like these, I explain what good or fun secrets are and what secrets could or would hurt them. A secret that hurts them or someone they love is not a good secret.

Children get to the point when they have had to tell so many people their story that they are tired of talking about it.

Understand this as a helper. Every time a child has to tell their story of abuse, it is exhausting and scary.

Telling a scary secret is very brave. Kids need to know this and understand they are brave for telling. They are also brave for getting help. It is scary to deal with trauma for anyone, especially a child. They have lost part of their innocence.

They lose a lot of things in telling their secret. They lose being able to trust adults. They lose being able to not be afraid. Children need to feel safe. They need to feel protected. I make sure when I am counseling children of trauma that they understand I will do what I need to do to help them feel safe.

Many times, they are scared their abuser will come find them. They may lie to keep themselves safe. They keep secrets to stay safe. They do not know who they can trust.

Kids of trauma just want to feel "normal." So, they may not say what is truly bothering them. They may refer to a step-parent as mom or dad. It is easier than having to explain the whole story yet again.

The secrets of trauma are embarrassing. Kids are ashamed of what has happened. They do not like to have to tell their story to a lot of people. They are angry, so they may hide what they are angry about.

Many times, when I ask a kid what they are angry about or worried about, they tell me "nothing." They do this for many reasons. They may not want to think about it so they say nothing or they truly may not know what they are worried or angry about. Try to help them work through this. Offer suggestions and a listening ear.

They may have just come back from a weekend with their other parent, where they had to be careful what they did or said. This puts a lot of stress on kids. They are constantly worried if they will get in trouble or upset someone.

The secrets of trauma are many. We need to help kids

understand some secrets are not okay or safe secrets to keep. We need to help them know who is safe to talk to and get help from. Kids who have experienced trauma have many secrets. Help kids talk about them and feel safe.

Change Happens

Change is part of life. No matter your age, change happens. You change schools, teachers, friends, houses, churches, jobs, and so on. Some changes are good and exciting ... some not so much. Some changes are downright devastating. Some changes dump your whole world upside down.

These changes are usually some kind of trauma or devastating event. This could be a loss, divorce, death, injury, financial hardship, and so on. These kinds of changes can be scary because they are unpredictable. They are usually unexpected and change many parts of your life.

Now, imagine you are a child. You do not have any control over the things happening to you and around you. You would be scared, probably angry, and definitely confused. Many times, because children tend to automatically blame themselves, they believe they did something wrong.

Children react to changes in many different ways. There could be regression in their development; for example, a child who was potty trained starts needing to wear diapers again or wetting the bed. Some children act out in their behavior. They become very angry in their actions. They also could become very withdrawn. They do not want to talk to anyone for many different reasons.

Changes which result from trauma are often life-altering. For example, in the case of divorce, it could mean moving to a different house and a different school. It could mean not seeing one parent as much or at all. It could mean stepparents and stepsiblings. That is a lot of change to happen all at once. It is hard on the adults; now imagine you are a little kid.

Kids who go through trauma or have been exposed to scary things like domestic violence or parents using alcohol or drugs is even harder. This is when other people get involved like a child protective services agency, the courts, a judge, the police, the foster care system, and any other agency you can think of.

Changes are scary in these cases. Children are removed from the ones they know. They are removed from siblings and friends. They have mixed emotions about their parents who leave them confused and often alone.

Helping a child who has gone through changes is not easy. In many cases, it takes a child several months or even years to fully adjust to the changes they have experienced. Sometimes they never really fully adjust to the changes and end up living in chaos well into adulthood. They develop coping mechanisms that are not helpful or healthy.

Helping children who have experienced trauma is something that is not easy. They are often scared, angry, and feel broken. They need to have help piecing their lives back together so they can move on. They need support, love, and compassion.

While life has its ups and downs for everyone, some people just seem to have a bad hand of cards dealt every time. They get easily frustrated and want to give up. They need to be taught how to make better choices in life so they can move beyond the trauma to not just survive, but to thrive.

Turn on Your Listening Ears

Do you have your listening ears on? I ask this question of kids all the time. It usually is asked when I can tell the child I am talking to is not listening to me or some other adult. They may be wiggling in their seat or talking or just not looking at me. Maybe, they are having a hard time focusing on things in general.

If we as adults expect children to listen to us, do we listen to them? Do we listen to them and what they want to talk about? Getting on a child's level is needed when talking with children—sometimes literally. Sometimes, it means you get on the floor or on their eye level to talk.

Show a child that you are engaged in the conversation. Show them that what they are talking about is important. It may be the same conversation from just a few minutes ago, or they are talking about Minecraft for the thousandth time.

Kids need to know they are being heard and are worth listening to when it comes to the small stuff and the big stuff. They will not talk to you about the big stuff if they feel you are not listening to the little stuff. They also will not go to another adult for help if they do not feel heard.

Take time to listen to them when they get home from school. Listen about their day and things going on at school. Ask if there are any problems at school or anywhere else. You know your child best. You want your child to come to you no matter what has happened.

When big, scary things happen in life, we want children to learn who the safe people are. They need to know who they can talk to and who will actually listen to them when they need it. Kids need to know their voice will be heard.

We as adults teach children to listen to us and do as they

are asked. We want children to follow directions and what they are told or asked to do. Do we as adults listen to children in the same way? Do we listen to children's wants and needs?

Most kids are not going to come home and say they had a bad day. They will most likely want to sit and cuddle or get our attention in some way. Every child needs to have one caring adult in their lives who listens to them no matter what they say or express. If a child is angry, talk to them about what is upsetting them. Acknowledge their feelings.

If they are scared, try to find out what is scaring them. Allow your child to express their emotions in a healthy way. Talk through how they feel and let them cry if they need to. Let them feel safe and loved when they talk with you.

Teaching kids the best way to express their feelings is the biggest thing that can be done to help a child. They need to know how to express themselves and know they will be heard. This is helping a kid to thrive, not just survive.

To Trust or Not to Trust, That Is the Question

Trust is such a little word but has such a big meaning. It can make or break a relationship. It can ruin lives. It can be so easily broken but so hard to rebuild. When we talk about trusting someone, there are different levels or types of trust for different relationships.

When we talk about a close relationship like a child and parent, trust seems to be built right in, or at least it should be. When we talk about a friendship, trust is built over time. It may take a lot of time before we trust others.

Children seem to have an easier time being able to trust others. They are innocent to life's hurt and pain that come with broken relationships. That is, unless they have experienced some kind of hurt or pain at a young age—something traumatic that can put a halt to them ever trusting anyone again. They have been hurt so many times, they do not dare trust anyone for fear of getting hurt again.

Usually, this kind of trust is broken in cases of abuse—any and all kinds of abuse. When the child is the victim and the abuser is a parent or close relative, trust just seems to evaporate. Many times, the child victim loves their parent, but trusting them is something completely different.

When a child is the victim of abuse, no matter the type, they struggle with trusting anyone. It takes longer for a child to trust anyone including, or especially, adults again. They have been hurt. They are scared they will be hurt again. Not trusting someone is their way of being able to keep safe.

When a child who has been abused does not trust adults, it is the job of the adult to take their time to allow the child to trust again. Take your time building a solid relationship with them. Keep your promises. Set your boundaries. Observe the child interacting with others.

When a child who has been traumatized comes into my office for the first time, I tell them that I do not expect them to spill their guts or tell me everything right away. They need to have time to get to know me and I them. Usually, after a few sessions, they can trust me enough and can begin to tell their secrets.

We need to take our time helping a child be able to thrive through trauma. Many times, when a child has been traumatized, they will at first act up in their behavior to see if you will leave them first. Try to push through this part. Have patience with them, sometimes a lot of patience. It is a way they protect themselves from further hurt.

Children who have been hurt need to know and feel safe

with the adults they are around. They need to know you will do your best to keep them safe. I set up ways for kids to communicate with me when they do not feel safe. I back off and give them time to collect themselves.

Trust is a big deal for kids who have experienced trauma. Do not take it personally if a child who has experienced trauma does not trust you right away. They have been hurt. Do not expect them to tell you everything right away. Go to the extent of asking if you can hug them. This gives them control and the ability to say no. They need to know you respect them and want to help them feel safe.

Being able to trust again is a big factor for many who have gone through trauma. This carries well into adulthood. Being a trusted adult is a big deal. Do not take it for granted or just expect it will happen with every child. Helping kids to thrive through trauma is helping them to trust people again. It is helping them to understand that not every person in their life is out to hurt them.

Trauma All Over Again, and Again, and Again

For some people, including kids, trauma just seems to be a way of life. They have one traumatic event after another. They have the same type of trauma over and over, for example, abuse. Some can have different traumatic events through their lifetime, for instance, abuse, a house fire, divorce, and an adverse medical diagnosis, all within a short period of time.

There are some people who are retraumatized so many times, it just becomes part of who they are. They do not know how to function any other way. They feel like a target. These people need intensive help. They need help dealing with the multiple things that have happened to them.

How to end this cycle or streak? First, remove yourself and your children from the situation. Second, reach out for help. Even if it is from a local agency. Seek professional help from a qualified mental health counselor.

If the trauma seems to be a generational problem, look around you to see what needs to change. Then try your best with the help of others to get help to get out of the situation. Maybe it is because you were abused as a child and do not know how to function outside of being in an abusive relationship.

Breaking the cycle may mean completely changing your environment. It may mean leaving relationships you have been in for years. It may mean setting limits with those around you who have poor boundaries themselves.

Helping someone to thrive and not just survive trauma is helping to break the cycle of trauma, which seems to happen in some families. It may mean saying "enough" and walking away.

Many times, the reason people stay in traumatic or abusive relationships is because they do not know any other way. Breaking away can be done if you are willing to try. Reaching out and working with others to help you is also key.

Helping kids to thrive through trauma is also helping their parents break the cycle of trauma, so it is not passed down to the next generation. This is not an easy task for anyone, but it is so worth it. Parents always want better for their children. Work on breaking the cycle of trauma in your family. This is thriving, not just surviving trauma.

Give Me Five!

We all need helpers in our lives. We all need to know who we can turn to when we need help. We also know who can help us with specific things. Having a support network is important not only for adults but also for children. They need to know who the safe people are.

One activity I do with the children I counsel is to have them spread out their hand. Sometimes we even trace it on paper. Then on each finger, the child lists an adult who is supportive and who they can trust to go to when they need help.

We try to list people in each place they go to on a regular basis, for example, a parent or other family member, a teacher, family friend, Sunday school teacher, pastor, coach, and so on. Some kids can tell me more than five. This is great. That means they have a lot of support. But some kids really struggle to list five.

We talk about what makes the adults they listed "safe." We talk about what kinds of things they could need help with. As you choose your list, let your child know they can talk to the adults they are close to, even if they cannot talk to you or are scared. They still have someone; they are not alone.

This is important to a child and a parent. My church kiddos know they can come to me if they need help and are struggling. Their parents also know if their child comes to me and something is wrong, I will contact them immediately. This is especially true if a child has experienced something scary or traumatic.

I explain to the kids who I come in contact with that part of my job as their therapist or children's ministry leader is to help them feel safe. If they do not feel safe, we need to figure it out so they do feel safe. Please be an adult who does this with the children and teens you come in contact with.

Many children and teens do not have "safe" adults in their lives. They feel alone and not wanted. I have had teens tell me they want to hurt themselves but are afraid to tell their parent for fear their parent will be angry with them. In this case, I usually talk to the parent with the teen, to be a support. Parents need to know, no matter if the teen wants to tell or not.

Helping a child thrive and not just survive trauma means being there for the scary stuff, not just the fun stuff. Children and teens need to know that even though there have been some bad things, they do have support and they are loved by someone. They have at least one caring adult in their corner, willing to fight for them and support them.

Being a helper or giving support to a traumatized child is not an easy job. It is downright messy. In the end, it is so worth it. Watching a child or teen overcome something that could have derailed their whole life is a very rewarding feeling for both you as the helper and the child you are helping. This is helping kids to thrive, not just survive, after trauma.

Chapter

8

Thriving vs. Surviving

Building Fences Not Walls

Kids love to build and make things. They love Legos and blocks to create something through their imagination. When they build something, they feel like they have control over what they are making.

Something all children need to learn is building and creating boundaries—setting limits with others. This is a part of healthy relationships. Creating personal space in our lives is important for so many reasons. Boundaries keep us safe.

When I talk with kids about setting boundaries, I explain it as building a fence. When we build a fence, we can still see people. We have control over the gate and who comes in and out of our space. Things can come in and out of the fenced-in area. When we have a fence, we can usually keep the bad stuff out.

Then there are kids who build walls. They build walls around themselves because they have been hurt. Some build their wall so high that no one can get in, even the people who love them. While walls do the job of keeping people out, they do not let any good things in.

Kids who have been hurt build their walls to keep themselves safe. They think this is going to help them. In the short term it does. They are safe from the person who hurt them, but they have isolated themselves from others who will not harm them.

While having boundaries is a good thing in relationships, isolating in general is not. Kids become very lonely very quickly. They do not have many friends. They do not have many adults in their lives they can trust.

Kids who have been hurt do not trust easily. We adults need to be patient with these kids. They need help, but they just do not know it or how to ask for it. Building walls is a way to survive. If they keep their walls up, they cannot get hurt.

It takes time for kids to bring down their walls. It is scary for them to do so. They are scared they will get hurt again. Kids need to learn to trust again. Not every person wants to hurt them.

Sometimes when helping kids with walls, bricks come down very slowly. They come down one at a time. We adults need to prove ourselves to these kids. We were not the ones who hurt them, but they believe that all adults will hurt or disappoint them at some point.

We need to help kids turn their walls into a fence. Show them that boundaries are important but so is having people in their life. Teaching kids who have been hurt to have proper boundaries is very important.

Teaching them boundaries helps them to thrive, not just survive. It's important that you as the adult also have boundaries. Part of setting boundaries is modeling them. It is okay to tell a child no. It is okay to set limits with children—they need them. They need to know where they stand with you.

Setting boundaries is part of any healthy relationship. Kids need to see what good boundaries are. They need to know what they can do and what they cannot do. Many times, kids have not been taught proper boundaries.

It is our job as adults to show and teach proper boundaries with others in our lives. Kids need to see this in action. This is helping kids to thrive, not just survive.

Turtles Are Tough and Soft

Anyone who knows me knows I collect turtles. Some may even say I am obsessed. If you walk into my home or my office, you will see turtles all over ... walls, shelves, beanies, pillows, wall hangings, and anywhere else you can think of. I collect them because they are just cool.

One of the reasons I think turtles are cool is because they are a reminder of how to be with others, especially ones who have hurt us or ones who have picked on us. I explain to kids to be a turtle and here is why.

Many of us like to share our feelings with others. But we can do this to the point of getting our feelings hurt very easily. We end up being a target for bullies. Bullies see people who are more sensitive as a target, someone they can pick on easily.

But if you are a turtle, that makes it more difficult for the bullies to get to you. You see, turtles have a hard outside shell. They use this shell for protection. The shell protects the turtle's vital organs as well as their softness. We do not want to be so hard-hearted in life that we do not want to help others.

We use our shells for protection when we need to but not all the time. We can take our time and take things slowly most of the time. We can go about life and help those around us as we are able. When we need it, however, we have our shell, and we can pull up into it for protection.

When it comes to our feelings, we need to protect them from those who mean to do harm. We protect our heart from those who seek to harm us just because they think they can.

The shell is the turtle's boundary. It says to others that you are going to stay inside your shell to protect yourself from harm or until the harm has passed. You may need to have your shell to protect you from people in your life who do harm or find it easy to pick on you.

Just because you have a shell does not mean you do not have feelings or that you cannot share your feelings with others. It just means that you are careful with whom you share them and in what situation.

God made turtles this way because He knows they are slow movers. A turtle can pull up inside its shell quickly if it feels threatened. The trick is to not stay in your shell for a long time. Come back out of your shell with the people you feel safe with and when you feel safe.

Helping kids or others with trauma is helping them come out of their shell. They have been in their shell for so long, they do not know when it is safe. They may poke their head out once in a while, but that may be very limited.

Helping others with trauma is being someone who is safe for them, someone with whom they can come out of their shell. This may be a slow process just like turtles move slowly, but it can be done. Turtles like to be out and play and swim and just live life like we do.

Help someone come out of their shell by being a safe person who they can trust and be themselves no matter what they are feeling. Be the person who can be trusted with the scary stuff and the hard stuff. Let the turtle come out and play.

Helping kids to thrive and not just survive after trauma is not an easy thing for anyone. For some people who have gone through trauma, it takes a lifetime to handle and deal with all the stress and scary things that happened. Be the safe person who can be trusted for them to come out of their shell. Be part of the healing process. This is so key in surviving and thriving after trauma.

Helping Them Succeed

Kids who are going through trauma or have gone through something traumatic seem to have been dealt a bad hand. The cards seem to be stacked against them. They are dealing with things at a young age that many people never deal with in their whole life.

They are raising their siblings. They are homeless. They are dealing with parents going to jail. Their parents are using substances. Kids are going hungry or without other basic needs that most of us take for granted.

There is a cycle to poverty and trauma. It just seems to go around and around with no way to stop it, but the cycle can be broken with the right help.

It takes people stepping in to help those who are struggling, to mentor them, and help them individually. It can start at a young age, in fact, the younger the better.

Helping kids with trauma who live below the poverty level usually means extra help and thinking outside the box. It might mean that items a child needs appear as if by magic. It may mean taking time to just sit and talk with a child to get to know them—their needs, their dreams, and their favorite things. Kids just want to be heard.

Most of what happens in the cycle of poverty is lack of employment or training to get decent jobs. Helping kids realize from a young age that education is important and a ticket to a better life is one way to help.

What does this look like for those wanting to help? Offer to tutor. Mom and dad may not be able to help with homework and schoolwork. Help a child by buying school supplies and clothes. When back-to-school supplies go on sale, pick up extra and share with a child in need. Kids should not have to worry about how they are going to do their schoolwork. They have bigger things going on than whether they have a pencil or not. This should be the least of their worries.

Make sure kids have food to eat when they are at school so they can focus better. If they need food, get them something to eat.

Help mom and dad with issues at home so kids have a safe

place to live. Provide safe places for kids to hang out after school so they can get extra help. Have people available to help and provide a listening ear when life is not going well.

Every kid needs someone in their corner. They need someone who is willing to fight for them. They need to have the tools to be successful in life. This is what will break the poverty and trauma cycles. This is helping kids to thrive, not just survive.

The Lost Boys and Girls

In the movie *Peter Pan*, there were the "lost boys" in Neverland. These were a group of boys who had no one to take care of them. While it seemed fun in the movie, in real life having a lost childhood is not fun. Losing childhood is not like losing a toy or money. It is much more valuable.

Childhood is supposed to be one of the best parts of your life. Some children, however, are pushed or forced to grow up too fast. They may be living in a single-parent family where they are expected to do more to help out. They may have had a traumatic event happen that stole their childhood innocence. A lost childhood may mean losing out on things like sports or other activities. It may mean having to take care of a parent when they are too drunk or high, because they cannot take care of themselves, let alone the other children in the house.

These lost children look around at their peers who seem to have a better life and just wish and dream that could happen to them. Their peers are going to ball games and social events, but they are stuck at home or being bounced around like a rubber ball from place to place because their parent just cannot seem to get it together.

The lost children may not even have an adult to depend on. Their parent may not even be around. They may be in and out of jail. They may be high or drunk. These are things a child should never have to see or deal with.

Many of these lost boys and girls just fall through the cracks. They try to find ways out of the situation they are in. Some, when they reach their teen years, run away or go live with friends or another family member just to get away. They know the choices their parents make are not good.

Helping kids in this situation is difficult, because they think there is no one who can help them. They think they have to take care of themselves. There is one problem with this—they are kids. Kids do not know how to take care of themselves or anyone else.

These lost children need caring adults who can step in and help them. Be the adult example they need to not just survive but thrive in life. If they have a basic need, try your best to meet their need.

There have been many times I have purchased food or clothes for a child in need. I feel this is my calling to do, when needed. God instructs us to help those who are in need.

Listen to these children. Many times, they are carrying such big burdens they just need to unload and have someone listen who is not judgmental. Many of these children are left to fend for themselves or to take care of their siblings. They may not have had much structure or rules so they could make a lot of poor choices. Help guide them in making better choices.

Helping kids to thrive through trauma means sometimes stepping in when and where someone else has stepped out, either physically or mentally or both. When a parent chooses not to parent their child for whatever reason, this can cause a lifetime of hurt and struggle. Give these lost children an adult they can look up to and strive to be an example of how to improve their life in the present and the future. Help them to feel not so lost in life.

A Promise is a Promise

Children seem to remember everything adults tell them. They remember the "promise" you made months ago or five minutes ago. They remember what you say or what you do. Kids are like little lie detectors. They can tell when someone is "lying" to them.

Unfortunately, for many children, they are lied to by trusted adults. I am not talking about an "I will buy you a treat at the store" kind of a lie. I am talking about an "I will pick you up and we will spend time together" kind of a lie. I am talking about not showing up for a school game or concert kind of a lie.

These promises get broken so many times that children just stop believing the person who is making the promises. Now, I understand some things cannot be helped. If you are going to make a promise, you better make sure you do your very best to make it work. Kids remember.

They begin to lose trust in all adults if one starts lying to them. If they cannot trust one adult, how can they trust another? This is kid logic. To some extent, they are right. Kids begin to think all adults lie. They trust adults so many times and so easily. When they stop trusting adults, we have a bigger problem.

Kids stop reaching out for help. They think no one cares about them. They believe all adults will hurt them when in reality, it is one adult who they trusted, like a parent, who has been breaking promises and lying to them.

When they are young, it is very easy for kids to trust adults. When this trust is broken over and over by the same person or the same promise gets made and broken, kids really struggle with believing adults.

When I make a promise to a kid, I explain to them that I will do my very best to keep my word. I explain and emphasize "if" I can make it work or make it happen. As someone who works with and loves children, I do my very best to keep my word. If I promise my church kids I am bringing doughnuts, I better deliver on my promise or they will not trust me with other things.

We tell kids all the time not to lie, but then adults do it. How is that fair? How is that right? It is not. If adults cannot be trusted with the little things like bringing doughnuts to class, then how can we be trusted with the big stuff?

To help a child to thrive and not just survive after trauma, we need to be adults of our word.

Loving Your Traumatized Child

Love is something every child, every person, needs. We were created by God to have human connection. God created us to be in a family and to love and be loved. When a child you love and care for has been hurt, your heart just breaks. You so badly want to fix their hurt and take it away.

Children who have experienced trauma need love and understanding just as much as, if not more than, their peers. Children who have experienced trauma have been hurt in a way that goes beyond a bump, a scrape, or a broken bone. They have been hurt on a level that many people will never truly understand.

Their young, innocent lives have been shattered by something that has changed them forever. Whether it is the death of a parent, abuse, divorce, abandonment, neglect, or some other life-altering event, their life has been broken into pieces.

Understanding this brokenness and what has happened to this child is the first step to loving them. Put yourself in their little shoes. Walk in their steps. See life from their view.

The second step is to help them rebuild their life. Help them to be able to push beyond whatever has changed them. Get them the help and resources they need so they can make steps in a positive direction.

The third step is to just be there. Love them. Reassure them. Over and over and over until they feel safe again. This could take years to happen. Be patient and consistent with them. They are emotionally fragile in their young lives. This makes them vulnerable. They need to know you are not going anywhere and that you are a safe person.

Loving a traumatized child is not an easy job. They have been hurt, many on a very personal level. They are not easily trusting. They do not want to get hurt again so they have learned to put up barriers to keep themselves safe. These barriers are hard to break down. It will take time. It will take patience. Loving a traumatized child is something we, all who love children, need to understand how to do.

They are out and about. They are in schools, churches, doctor's offices, and everywhere you are. They do not wear a label that says, "I have had trauma." These children are looking for love, sometimes in the wrong places. We need to protect them and be aware of what is going on around them to keep them safe. We need to help teach them to keep themselves safe. All children need love, but some are just harder to love than others. The ones who are hard to love are usually the ones who need it most.

Loving a traumatized child is something we as adults, caregivers, and parents need to learn how to do. If it does not affect your child, it has affected their friend, your friend's child, or another child who comes into your life. They have come into your life for a reason—because they need love.

Worry Less, Play More

Kids worry—some more than others. They worry about tests at school. They worry about friends and family. They worry about bullies. They worry about grown-up things like bills and money. Some things are not kid worries. This is what I tell the kids I counsel.

When kids worry and stress about things over a long period of time, or they seem to worry about things they have no control over or things that could not realistically happen, this is cause for adults to be concerned. This means your child has anxiety or is on the edge of developing it.

When kids have gone through trauma, they become stressed and overwhelmed very easily. They seem to always be functioning in crisis mode. They are continually trying to fix grown-up problems. Kids who worry like this are in some ways forced to grow up faster than they should.

Kids who have gone through trauma worry if they or a loved one will be hurt again. They worry about having enough to eat, a place to live, and clothes to wear. They worry if their parent will be alive in the morning because their parent was using drugs the night before. They worry if there will be another accident or illness.

What kids need to relieve this stress is reassurance. They need to know there are grown-ups who can handle the worries they are thinking about. Kids need to know they will be safe and protected from harm. They need to know they will have food to eat and a place to live.

Helping kids to thrive and not just survive means helping them worry less and play more. Kids need the freedom to be kids. They need to know they are cared for. They need to know adults can handle their adult problems and take care of their children too. Kids need to feel safe and protected on every level. This is the job of an adult.

Helping kids to thrive and not just survive means to help them through their stressors of life, no matter what that means. Children need to be loved unconditionally. They need reassurance when bad stuff happens. They need to know who they can go to for help and guidance. This is helping kids to thrive, not just survive trauma and life.

Life happens. Bad things happen. No matter how much we as adults try to protect them, stuff happens. We need to be safety nets children can fall into when life goes wrong. They need to know it is going to be okay, no matter what.

Photo by Megan and Jody Terrell/Wallhanger Photography in Gainsville, Georgia.

About the Author

Alison Neihardt is a Licensed Professional Counselor (LPC) with a private practice in northern Michigan, where she grew up. Alison works with children, teens, and their parents. She holds a master of arts in counseling from Spring Arbor University. She also earned a bachelor of science in counseling and an associate of arts in early childhood education from Great Lakes Christian College in Lansing, Michigan. Alison has worked in private practice since 2008 with children from ages three to seventeen, many whose parents abused drugs and/or alcohol and are being raised by their grandparents for a variety of reasons. Alison has also worked as a volunteer and in paid ministry positions in churches and parachurch organizations. She began writing to help others in 2016. Her first book, *Counseling Activities for Children on a Shoestring Budget*, was published in the spring of 2019.

Made in the USA
Monee, IL
21 July 2022